TRIED AND TRUE

RECIPES

==

PUBLISHED BY THE PRESBYTERIAN
LADIES' AID SOCIETY
OF PRINEVILLE

1909

REPUBLISHED BY THE
CROOK COUNTY HISTORICAL SOCIETY
BOWMAN MUSEUM
246 N. MAIN ST. 447-3715
PRINEVILLE, OREGON 97754

1987

10-13 PRINT SHOP
PRINTERS
PRINEVILLE, ORE.

Organization of the Aid Society

President . . . . . . Mrs. Mary Lister

Vice-President . . . . Mrs. E. True Shattuck

Secretary . . . . . . Mrs. Anna L. Winnek

Treasurer . . . . . . Mrs. Ida Morse

Publishing Committee

Mrs. Mary J. Wigle   Mrs. Anna L. Winnek

Mrs. Annie Babbidge

TO THOSE

PLUCKY HOUSEWIVES

WHO MASTER THEIR WORK INSTEAD
OF ALLOWING IT TO MASTER THEM,

THIS BOOK IS DEDICATED

CONTENTS

SOUPS

"Now good digestion waits on appetite, and health on both."

All soup meat should be put on in cold water and simmered several hours; stand over night and skim off all grease before using.

Cream Celery Soup.—Heat three pints of soup stock, and to this add one cup of celery; cut in small pieces; fry a small piece of onion in one tablespoonful of butter until yellow; add one tablespoonful of flour and slowly add enough of the stock soup to make it thin enough to pour. Put this with the soup, pour through a sieve, cook ten minutes, then add one pint of hot cream. Season with salt and pepper, sprinkle with minced parsley and serve.

MRS. AMANDA ELKINS.

Cream of Celery Soup.—No. 1.—Cut a bunch of celery into dice and cook till tender in a little water; melt a heaping tablespoon butter and add tablespoon flour; cook till it smells done, but do not brown: add a scant quart of rich milk and the cooked celery and water; bring to a boil and season well with salt and pepper.

MRS. J. H. W.

Cream of Celery Soup—No. 2.—Heat three pints of white soup stock, and to this add one cup of celery, cut in dice, and parboil in water to cover; fry one tablespoonful of minced onion in one table-spoonful butter until yellow; add one tablespoonful of flour and slowly add enough of the soup stock to make it thin enough to pour; put this with the soup, pour through a sieve, cook ten minutes, then add one pint hot cream. Season with salt and pepper, sprinkle with minced parsley and serve.

MRS. CROOKS.

Tomato Soup—No. 1.—One can tomatoes; salt and pepper; 2 bay leaves; 3 or 4 cloves; 2 or 3 red peppers; 1 teaspoonful sugar; let this come to boil; strain; add 1 pint hot water; thicken with tablespoonful of flour.

MRS. B. F. J.

Macaroni Soup.—To a rich beef or other soup in which there is no seasoning other than pepper or salt, take half a pound of small pipe macaroni, boil it in clear water until it is tender, then drain it and cut it in pieces of an inch length; boil it for fifteen minutes in the soup and serve.

MRS. McF.

Tomato Soup.—Two tablespoonfuls flour, two tablespoonfuls butter; warm butter in frying pan, adding slowly to flour; work these together until flour thickens, then add one quart of canned tomatoes with a large slice of onion, salt, pepper and one cup of water. Cook about ten minutes. Just before serving put through a sieve and add a cup of cream.

LILLIAN MADDEN.

Cream Tomato Soup—No. 2.—Put one quart of tomatoes through a colander; add a pint of boiling water, let come to a boil and add a pinch of soda, a pint of cream, a lump of butter and salt and pepper to taste; must not boil after cream is added.

EMMA EDWARDS.

Potato Soup.—Peel and slice 3 or 4 medium sized potatoes and one onion, 1 small slice bacon cut in dice; cover with cold water and cook till tender; put through strainer if desired and add 1 pint rich milk, butter size of walnut; salt and pepper to taste.

MRS. J. H. W.

Oyster Soup.—Place 1 quart of sweet milk in a double boiler, add the liquor from a can of oysters and heat to the boiling point, but do not boil; add salt and pepper and a lump of butter the size of an egg, also a few cracker crumbs; add oysters and remove from the fire at once and serve.

MRS. C. A. RIDDLE.

Vegetable Soup.—To 2 quarts of beef broth, not too greasy, add 1 good sized onion; 1 medium sized potato; 1 small handful of rice; a carrot and a little finely chopped cabbage may be added; season to taste.

MRS. W. H. PROSE.

Cream Tomato Soup.—One can of tomatoes, quart can; 2 quarts water; boil water and tomatoes for one hour; strain through a sieve and to this add one-quarter pound of butter, one-half teaspoonful soda, 1 quart of new milk, boiled; lastly, add pepper and salt. Salt will curdle new milk, hence add it last.

MRS. E. F. LONG.

Noodles for Beef Soup.—Beat up one egg, add a little salt and a pinch of baking powder and enough flour to make a very stiff dough; roll out very thin and sprinkle over with flour; roll up tight, and slice off in very thin slices and sprinkle with a little flour to keep from sticking and drop into the boiling soup and boil five minutes, is sufficient; if boiled too long they go to pieces.

JULIA YOUNG.

Rice Tomato Soup.—Save soup stock from a boil of beef or mutton or from a soup bone, let stand over night, skim off all grease, add an onion about the size of an egg and 3 or 4 large tomatoes, or about half a quart of canned ones; cook all together till onion and tomato are soft, remove from fire and strain; then add handful of rice well washed, season with salt and pepper and add water enough to serve 6 people; cook till rice is thoroughly done. This is especially good.

MRS. JOHN WIGLE.

Vegetable Soup.—Save soup stock from a boil of beef, mutton or soup bone, let it stand over night and skim off all grease; this is the secret of all good soups; chop fine an onion, potato, turnip, a little cabbage, parsley, celery, green pepper; add these and some tomatoes, a cupful or more if desired, to the cold stock; cook till vegetables are tender, remove from fire and strain, and then add a few slices of carrot cut very thin or in fancy shapes; cook till tender; season well with pepper and salt. Water should be added to soup stock enough to serve several people. One can use all vegetables named or omit any if not to be obtained. The dry celery leaves and dry parsley are very nice and hardly to be told from the fresh. The soup is more dainty strained, but some prefer to leave in the vegetables.

FANNY RAY JOHNSON.

8

FISH

*"The silvery fish, grazing in meadows submarine,
Fresh from the wave now cheers our festive board."*

Creamed Salmon.—1 can salmon minced fine; drain off liquor and discard; melt 2 tablespoonfuls butter, add 2 tablespoonfuls flour and stir and cook together; add rapidly 1 pint of milk; salt to taste; have ready 1 pint fine bread crumbs or cracker crumbs; place a layer in the bottom of a buttered pudding dish, add a layer of fish, then one of cream gravy, alternating until the dish is full, having a layer of crumbs on top; beat up an egg, add a little milk, and pour over the top layer. Dot the top thickly with butter, bake a delicate brown, about 20 minutes.

M. L.

Spiced Salmon.—Cut salmon in small pieces about 2 inches square; cover in cold water, put on stove, cook slowly and let come to boiling point (do not boil); pour off water and let cool; then place in stone or granite vessel in alternate layers with sliced onions and lemons and the following spices, cinnamon sticks, whole cloves, whole alspice, and bay leaves, with a dash of cayenne pepper and mustard; when vessel is filled, pour over the following mixture: cider vinegar (not too strong), to which add two tablespoonfuls of brown sugar to one quart of vinegar, and 4 tablespoonfuls of olive oil; salt to taste. Let stand about one and one-half days before using. Salt salmon can be prepared in the same way by freshening in water one and a half days.

Ada B. Millican.

Escalloped Clams.—Seven crackers soaked in milk; one-third cup butter; 1 can clams with juice, 2 eggs well beaten; salt and pepper; put in covered dish and bake three-quarters of an hour.

M. A. E.

Creamed Fish.—One pint fish; 1 tablespoon melted butter; 1 level teaspoon flour; 1 small cup cream; one-half cup celery; salt and pepper. Either serve on toast or in cases.

Cases for Cream Fish.—One egg; one-half teaspoon salt; one-half teaspoon sugar; 1 tablespoon olive oil; nearly one-half cup flour; three-fourths gill milk; make batter and fry in timbale irons. Makes 12 to 15.

Mrs. Morse.

Salmon Loaf.—Six crackers, rolled; 1 egg; 3 tablespoons cream; pepper and salt to taste; 1 can salmon; mold in loaf and bake.

Mrs. Collins W. Elkins.

9

White Sauce for Fish.—One tablespoon butter; 1 tablespoon flour; one-half teaspoon salt; one-fourth teaspoon pepper; 1 cup hot milk. Melt flour and butter without browning, add the salt and pepper and hot milk. Let simmer for a few minutes. Add a hard boiled egg, chopped fine, and a little parsley.

MRS. E. J. BURROWS.

Baked Trout—(Original).—Melt a little butter in a baking pan; lay in the prepared trout, first seasoning with salt and pepper, and roll them in flour; put bits of butter over them and inside them and pour a generous amount of tomato catsup over and inside them; add a very little water and bake till done. The trout 10 to 15 inches long are best and will cook in half an hour.

MRS. JOHN WIGLE.

Fish Cakes.—Save fish left from dinner, and use while warm; remove skin and bones, and mix with mashed potatoes; add pepper, salt, chopped parsley, and an ounce of butter; moisten with egg into a paste, and roll into balls; then flatten and dip into beaten eggs; fry in butter to a nice brown.

MRS. L. BIGGS.

Clams on Toast.—Chop fine 24 clams; melt two tablespoons butter and add 2 tablespoons flour; then add clams with one-half pint of their juice; season well and let simmer 15 minutes. Just before serving add 1 cup cream, let come to a boil. Serve on **hot** toast.

L. B.

Cream Salmon.—One can salmon minced fine; drain off liquid and discard; melt two tablespoons of butter; add two tablespoons flour; stir and cook together; add rapidly one pint of milk; salt to taste; have one pint bread or cracker crumbs, place layer of fish, then of cream gravy alternately until dish is full, having a layer of crumbs on top; beat up an egg, add a little milk and pour over top layer; dot the top thickly with bits of butter. Requires about twenty minutes to bake.

MRS. CROOKS.

Salmon Dressing.—Half cup vinegar; 2 teaspoons sugar; 1 teaspoon salt; 1 teaspoon flour; mix all together, stir until boils; add 2 teaspoons cream, sweet or sour; one egg, boiled, mashed and stirred in; boil two eggs and cut in dressing when cold; pepper and mustard to taste.

OLLIE ELKINS STEWART.

Salmon Turbot.— One can salmon; 3 eggs one-half cup bread or cracker crumbs; 4 teaspoons melted butter; seasoned with salt, pepper and parsley, beat fish and butter until smooth; beat bread crumbs and eggs, then put all together; put in buttered mould and bake 1/2 hour at 400°.

Sauce for Turbot.—One cup milk, heated to boiling, thickened with 1 tablespoon of cornstarch; juice of salmon; one large tablespoon of butter; one teaspoon catsup; a little parsley; pepper; one egg, beaten and put in; then very carefully let all just come to a boil. Serve on hot platter and pour sauce over turbot just before sending to the table.

MRS. M. R. ELLIOTT.

Baked Salmon.—Take nice piece of salmon, wash and dry in a cloth; salt and pepper, and bake in open pan, not cover; pour water in pan, put lump of butter on fish; baste often; cook well.

Sauce for Salmon.—Put rich milk on stove, as much as needed; thicken with flour; 1 boiled egg for each person, chopped fine; salt, pepper, and lemon added to suit taste.

Mrs. A. Thomson.

Oyster Patties.—Line patty pans with thin pastry, pressing it well to the tin, or invert pans and bake crust on inverted side; bake extra squares of crust to place on top of patties before serving. The shells may be baked the day before using and reheated; scald as many fresh oysters as you require, or use the canned ones; put 2 tablespoonfuls of butter and 2 of flour into a saucepan; stir them over the fire till the flour smells cooked; be careful not to scorch; then pour one-half pint of oyster liquor and one-half pint milk into the flour and butter (if you have cream, use it in place of milk); stir till it is a thick, smooth sauce; cut the oysters into bits and let them boil up once; beat the yolks of 2 eggs, remove mixture from fire and stir in the eggs; set on back of stove and cook till sauce looks like thick custard; fill shells with hot mixtures, place square on top. Delicious.

Mrs. John Wigle.

MEATS

"Some hae meat and canna eat
And some would eat that want it,
But we hae meat, and we can eat,
Sae let the Lord be thankit."

Chop Suey.—One layer stock of celery and four large onions fried until tender in three tablespoons of butter; boil one and one-half pounds of lean pork steak cut in small pieces, until tender, when it should have about a cup of liquor on it; turn this into the celery and onion, salt and pepper to taste; 2 tablespoons of Worcestershire sauce, and last 1 can of mushrooms. Serve with a border of boiled rice.

MRS. LOUIS DOONER.

Pot Roast Beef.—Take a lean piece of beef, cut a little piece of fat off from it, and fry in an iron pot for a few minutes; season the beef and sprinkle over a little flour; put in pot and fry brown on all sides; pour in hot water to half cover the beef; cover tightly and cook until tender; add a little boiling water at intervals to prevent burning; thicken the gravy and pour around the meat on the platter.

MRS. E. F. LONG.

Scalloped Sweetbreads.—Salt to taste; butter size of an egg; one cup milk; two pairs of sweetbread; yolks of three eggs; one cup bread crumbs; parboil sweetbread and throw into cold water. One pair sufficient for two or three; cut up sweetbread, mix with milk and eggs (yolks), butter, bread crumbs and the salt; bake in a dish.

MRS. G. N. CLIFTON.

Saddle of Mutton With Peas.—Dredge a saddle of mutton with salt, pepper and flour; roast with the flank ends up one hour, basting often; turn, and brown the upper part twenty minutes; drain and rinse a can of peas, cover with boiling water, and drain again; add teaspoonful of sugar, half a teaspoonful of salt and two tablespoonfuls of butter.

MRS. CROOKS.

Roast Lamb or Mutton.—Wash your roast and put in baking pan; salt and pepper it; slice an onion over the top; this prevents any unpleasant flavor that it might have; cover it over and put on top of stove; when it boils, add a pod of red pepper broken up and half a cupful of food vinegar, then put inside and roast, basting it as it cooks. Cook thoroughly done.

MRS. CROOKS.

Calves Brains.—Take calf brains and soak one hour in cold water; parboil and when cold, cut into pieces about the size of an oyster, dip in egg and bread crumbs and fry in boiling lard or dip in egg rolled in corn meal. Serve with slices of lemon.

MRS. CLIFTON.

Stuffed Calves Heart.—Cut central muscles out; cover with equal parts vinegar and water, adding one teaspoonful of salt; six cloves; one-half of bay leaf; soak two days and simmer until tender; stuff with highly seasoned bread dressing, brown in a hot oven, pour thickened gravy about the base; garnish with sprigs of tender young parsley.

MRS. CLIFTON.

The Bean Pot Roast.—Purchase about two pounds of stew meat; cut this into pieces about two inches square and put into the bean-pot; add half a teaspoonful of salt, but nothing else, adjusting the cover at once and setting the pot inside the stove; bake two hours, not lifting the lid. Send to table in bean pot. This simple dish may be varied in many ways. Half an hour before time to serve it, half a can of tomatoes may be added, or potatoes and small onions. Chicken, quail and many kinds of game may be cooked in a bean pot.

MRS. G. N. CLIFTON.

Liver Loaf.—Boil a lamb's liver until tender in water to which has been added an onion and a stalk of celery, salt and pepper; when cold wipe the liver dry and put through meat grinder; rub it to a paste with half a teaspoonful onion juice, a teaspoonful of Worcestershire sauce, one of mushrooms, ketchup and three of melted butter and two tablespoonfuls of olive oil and a dash of cayenne pepper. Butter a small, straight mold and press the liver mixture down into it. Leave on ice till just before serving—cut in thin slices and serve.

MRS. CLIFTON.

Little Pigs in Blankets.—Take as many large oysters as desired; wash and dry them thoroughly; season with salt and pepper; cover each oyster with a thin slice of bacon and pin together with a wooden toothpick; have the frying pan hot; cook just long enough to crisp the bacon; place on hot buttered toast and serve at once.

E. TRUE SHATTUCK.

Veal Loaf (No. 1).—Three and one-half pounds of minced veal; three eggs well beaten; one tablespoonful of pepper and one of salt; four rolled crackers; one tablespoon of cream; butter size of an egg; mix these together and make into a loaf; roast and baste like other meats. Beef may be used in place of veal by adding one-fourth pound of salt pork, minced fine.

R. B.

Veal Loaf (No. 2).—Three pounds veal; 2 pounds pork; grind up together; 1 egg, well beaten; 4 crackers, minced fine; one-half cup milk, salt and pepper; put in dripping pan in loaf; put in little water; bake in moderate oven. This is very fine.

OLLIE ELKINS STEWART.

Begue Stew.—One large spoon lard, very hot; 3 pounds veal cut in finger lengths, well browned; take out meat and slice 6 medium sized onions, and brown in grease, adding a little more lard if necessary; when onions are browned, add 2 tablespoons flour and brown; add water and stir until there is a good gravy; add meat; let simmer 4 to 5 hours; when half done, season with salt and pepper and 2 bay leaves. When ready to serve add can of peas and yolk of egg, if desired.

Mrs. J. M. Lawrence.

Hamburg Loaf.—Two pounds of raw beef; 1 pound of pork, chopped fine; 1 cup cracker or bread crumbs; 2 eggs; 1 cup sweet milk; piece of butter size of walnut, salt, pepper and 1 onion chopped fine; Mix well and bake 2 hours.

E. True Shattuck.

Roast Beef.—Take a rib piece or loin roast of seven or eight pounds; wash thoroughly; put it on a roast-pan and baste it well with butter or suet fat; set it in a well-heated oven; baste it frequently with its own drippings; when partly done, season with salt and pepper, then dredge with sifted flour.

Mrs. McFarland.

Mint Sauce for Mutton or Lamb.—Four dessert spoonfuls of chopped mint leaves; 2 dessert spoonfuls of white sugar; one-fourth pint of vinegar; dissolve sugar in vinegar and pour over mint leaves; stir well and let stand 3 or 4 hours before using.

Mrs. Jack Sumner.

Roast Turkey. With Oyster Dressing.—Dress and rub turkey thoroughly inside and out with salt and pepper; steam or boil two hours or until tender, lifting the cover occasionally and sprinkling lightly with salt; then take out and stuff with a dressing prepared as follows: Take a loaf of stale bread, cut off crust and soften by placing in a pan, pouring on boiling water, draining off immediately and covering closely crumble the bread fine, add half a pound melted butter, and a teaspoon each of salt and pepper, a tablespoon of chopped parsley; drain off liquor from a quart of oysters, bring to a boil, skim and pour over the bread crumbs, adding the soaked crusts and two eggs; mix all thoroughly, and if rather dry moisten with a little sweet milk; lastly, add the oysters, being careful not to break them or first put in a spoonful of stuffing and then three or four oysters, and so on until the turkey is filled; stuff the breast first; sew up closely and place in a dripping pan; turn until nicely browned on all sides.

Martha J. Wigle.

Fried Veal Cutlets.—Season veal with salt and pepper, dip in well beaten egg; then dredge with rolled crackers or dried bread crumbs, rolled fine and nicely seasoned with salt and pepper; if crackers are used, heat in oven to remove moisture before rolling; put to fry in boiling hot grease; brown nicely on both sides. Fish may be fried in the same way; when done the meat will separate readily from the bone when a knife is inserted; they may be dipped in milk, then in flour, instead of in egg and bread crumbs.

Mrs. J. D. L.

15

The Fireless Cooker

No longer an experiment, but an assured success. It saves enough time, fuel, wear and tear on your nerves to pay for itself within ten days.

Ours are factory-made—beautifully finished in dull black mission.

The W. F. KING COMPANY
PRINEVILLE, ORE.

Beef Rissoles.—The remains of cold roast beef minced very fine; to each pound of beef allow three-fourths pound of bread crumbs, salt and pepper to taste; a few chopped savory herbs; one-half teaspoon minced lemon peel; 1 or 2 eggs, according to the quantity of beef. Mix all together and form into balls and fry a rich brown; garnish with parsley or brown some flour in the grease and make a good gravy, to pour around rissoles on platter.

Mrs. Jack Sumner.

Roast Beef with Yorkshire Pudding.—Bake as directed for ordinary roasts for the table; for pudding the ingredients are, one pint of milk; four eggs, whites and yolks beaten separately; one teaspoon of salt; and two teaspoonfuls of baking powder, sifted through two cups of flour; it should be mixed very smooth, about the consistency of cream; take two common biscuit tins, dip some of the drippings from the dripping pan into these tins, pour half of the pudding into each, bake in hot oven; some pour pudding around, and under roast to cook; cook pudding half an hour or forty minutes, before dishing up meat.

Mrs. J. D. L.

Hamburger Steak.—Take a pound of raw flank or round steak; chop it until a perfect mince; also chop a small onion quite fine and mix well with the meat; season with salt and pepper; make into cakes as large as a biscuit, but quite flat; have ready a frying pan with butter and lard mixed; when boiling hot put in the steak and fry brown; a brown gravy made from the grease the steak was fried in and poured over the meat enriches it.

Mrs. McF.

Sliced Beef (Very Nice).—Boil a shank of beef in as little water as will cover it; cook till meat falls from bones; chop very fine; spice with ground cloves, pepper, salt and summer savory; add sufficient of the liquor in which it was cooked to moisten well; press into moulds and when cold slice.

L. Biggs.

Beef Patties.—Chop fine some cold beef; beat 2 eggs and mix with meat, adding a little milk, melted butter, salt and pepper; make into rolls and fry.

Mrs. George Stanclift.

Beefsteak Smothered with Onions.—Season steak with pepper and salt and dredge with flour; then place in good hot grease and spread over the top a thin layer of onions cut very fine; cover with a lid that fits closely; cook a few minutes over a good hot fire; turn the steak over and cover tight again for a few minutes more. Serve very hot.

Mrs. W. H. Young.

Meat Hash.—Take bits of cold roast meat of any kind, fried steak, sausage or chops, either pork or mutton; take out all bone, gristle and skin; put through grinder; put in pan and cover with water; season well with red pepper and salt and onion if liked; let cook 15 minutes and thicken with flour. A mixture of meats is best. Served with boiled rice is nice.

Mrs. J. H. W.

17

Canned Beef.—Carve all meat off bone and cut in small pieces; pack jars half full, then add salt sufficient to season; add meat to fill jars packed solid; place lids on jars, but do not tighten; place boiler on stove with cold water; put jars in and boil 4 hours; remove jars and seal tight and boil again one-half hour; do not let water boil over tops of jars, and don't wash meat before canning as any water will spoil its keeping. This is an excellent way to keep meat and is delicious, warm or cold. Broth may be poured off and by adding water, butter and seasoning to taste, makes excellent dumplings, dressings, soups, etc.

MRS. F. ROWEL.

Mother's Hash.—Put through grinder or chop fine bits of cold beef or mutton; take three-fourths or equal amount of cold boiled potatoes, not mashed; chop fine and mix with meat; have frying pan hot with a little dripping or bacon fat; add hash, pour over a little water, season with salt and pepper and a little celery salt, if liked, and onion also, if desired. Cook down and let brown well, but do not stir after it begins to brown. Run a knife around and under, roll up or turn half over in shape of a roll, turn out on hot platter.

FANNY R. JOHNSON.

Fricasseed Chicken, Southern Style.—Cut up a good fat hen, put on in hot water, let simmer slow until ready to drop from bones; just before it is done season well with salt and pepper; thicken the broth and have ready some rich baking powder biscuits; cut small or if large ones, break them, lay on platter and pour chicken and gravy over them.

MRS. RIPLEY.

Pot Roast of Beef or Veal.—Take 4 or 5 pounds beef or veal, season well with salt and pepper and dredge thoroughly with flour; melt one-half teacupful each of tallow and butter in a good sized granite kettle and heat until steaming hot; then add meat and brown nicely on all sides; add a quart of boiling water, cover and let boil moderately for about three hours. When done the gravy will be brown and ready to serve.

MRS. C. A. RIDDLE.

Meat Pasties.—Take a quarter's worth of good, tender beefsteak; cut into small pieces; half that amount of finely chopped potatoes; one small onion; season well with salt and pepper, and mix well together. Make a crust of one cup of finely chopped suet, one teaspoon of salt and flour, water enough to make a dough; divide the dough, take half the prepared meat, put in the dough and roll, cutting small holes in top of crust.

DORA THRONSON.

Presbyterian Chicken Pie.—Joint fowl; cover with boiling water; when half done season well with pepper and salt, and cook till ready to fall from bones; when able to handle, cut into bits, removing gristle and bones; add chicken to broth and thicken to make nice gravy; add water if necesary, adding butter to taste; if chicken is too fat, skim off grease before thickening; make a good rich crust, not so rich as for pie, adding 1 teaspoonful baking powder to 1 pint flour; bake with or without bottom crust; bake in individual pans, but do not borrow ours.

PRESBYTERIAN LADIES' AID.

18

Meat Pie.—Cut a round steak into finger lengths; season with salt and pepper; roll in flour and fry brown in lard or drippings; when brown put pieces of meat in stew kettle, cover with hot water, add a little minced onion if desired, and set on back of stove and simmer several hours, remembering that "a stew boiled is a stew spoiled." When meat is ready to drop to pieces, thicken broth till it makes a nice gravy, adding water if necessary. This is nice served as a stew or put into a pan and covered with a nice crust made a little richer than for biscuit and baked a nice brown. A few tomatoes, carrots or potatoes added are nice or all three, if served as a stew.

MRS. JOHN WIGLE.

19

SPECIALS

VEGETABLES

"Cheerful looks makes every dish a feast."

Baked Beans, with Tomato Catsup (No. 1).—Soak three cups of white beans over night; then add two-thirds cup catsup; three table-spoonfuls brown sugar; one-half pound salt; pork, cut in dice; salt and pepper to taste. Bake five hours in moderate oven.

MRS. CROOKS.

Baked Beans (No. 2).—Soak 3 cups of beans over night; in morning parboil with pinch of soda, or soaking may be omitted if parboiled till skin is ready to slip; place slice of pickled pork in bottom of bean crock; mix beans with 2 tablespoons black molasses, 1 of brown sugar, and season well with pepper and salt; put in crock and cover with water; place generous slice of pork or bacon on top. Bake till soft, adding water when necessary.

FANNY R. JOHNSON.

Cabbage and Potatoes.—Soak cabbage in salt water about 15 minutes, then cook cabbage and when soft chop fine; take 1 tablespoonful of good drippings and cut up a piece of onion and brown; then add the cabbage and 4 or 5 medium sized potatoes and season with salt, pepper and enough water to cover. Cook till tender.

B. MICHEL.

Scalloped Potatoes.—Sliced potatoes cut thin; place in pan, add salt, pepper and 1 pint of sweet cream; sprinkle flour over the top; bake in hot oven covered until last ten minutes.

WILDA BELKNAP.

Warmed Up Potatoes.—Two cups of mashed potatoes; add two well beaten eggs; place in pan and sprinkle pepper on top, also little bits of pieces of butter. Bake 20 minutes in hot oven.

WILDA BELKNAP.

Stuffed Cabbage.—Take small crisp head of cabbage, leave whole; pull each leaf back separately; then take brown bread crumbs fried in butter and put between the leaves; put in a cloth and draw tightly together. Tie; boil in salt water until done.

MRS. B. F. J.

Cabbage, English Style.—Separate leaves of a good solid head of cabbage, each leaf should be separate; add one-fourth teaspoon soda and teaspoon salt and a little water; cook till tender, drain and season with butter or serve with meat gravy.

MRS. E. J. BURROWS.

Fresh Peas.—Wash a few lettuce leaves and lay them in a sauce pan; wash peas and add them with just a very little water, as lettuce will form enough moisture. Cook till tender, remove lettuce leaves and season with butter.

MRS. E. J. BURROWS.

Delicious Roasting Ears.—Husk the ears all but the inner leaves; lay in kettle and pour boiling water over them; let boil about ten minutes; remove from fire and remove the husk or serve with the husk on.

MRS. J H. W.

Carrots, German Style.—Scrape and slice very thin; put on to cook with just a little water, tablespoon butter, salt and pepper. Cook till tender, adding water if necessary, but when done should be just about dry; add tablespoon good tart vinegar and let boil about 5 minutes.

MRS. J. H. WIGLE.

Escalloped Turnips.—Pare, slice and boil until tender in salt water; drain and put in baking dish; cover with cream sauce; dust with buttered crumbs and brown in quick oven.

MRS. COLLINS W. ELKINS.

Stewed Beets.—Boil them first and then scrape and slice them; put them into a stew pan with a piece of butter rolled in flour; some boiled onions and parsley chopped fine and a little vinegar, salt and pepper; set the pan on the fire and let the beets stew for fifteen minutes.

F. N.

Scrambled Tomatoes.—Remove the skins from a dozen tomatoes; cut them up in a sauce pan; add a little butter, pepper and salt; when thoroughly done beat up five or six eggs just before you serve them onto the pan with tomatoes and stir one way for two minutes, allowing them to be done thoroughly.

F. N.

Succotash.—Take a quart of string beans; if the beans are pretty well grown in the pods they are better; string and break into small pieces; put on in sufficient water to cover and boil for half an hour; then drain off the water and just cover again with boiling water; then add a few thin slices of bacon or ham fat and boil till the beans are tender; then add about one and a half pints of corn cut from the cob and boil about fifteen minutes; season with salt and pepper about half a cup of milk and butter to taste and a teaspoonful of flour moistened with milk. Serve while good and hot. Remove the meat before serving.

MRS. JULIA YOUNG.

Escalloped Potatoes.—Peel and slice raw potatoes; then butter porcelain pan; put in a layer of potatoes, and season with salt, pepper, butter and a bit of onion chopped fine; sprinkle with flour; now put another layer of potatoes and the seasoning; continue in this way until the dish is filled; just before putting into the oven, pour a quart of hot milk over; bake three-quarters of an hour.

Another recipe exactly like this, omits the onion and adds grated cheese and a dash of red pepper. Delicious.

R. B.

BREAD

"The very staff of life, the comfort of the husband and the joy of the wife."

(Light bread should never be overheated or hurried while raising. It should be put in a good warm oven so as to brown the first 15 minutes. Cover and bake slowly from 60 to 90 minutes. When done turn out on board where cold air will strike it. Individual loaves are the best.)

Bread.—For 3 loaves of bread use about one and one-fourth pints warm water; tablespoonful salt and about a cupful or a little more of dry potato yeast; use flour sufficient to make a very stiff batter, just about as stiff as can be stirred; set at night, keep in a warm place; in the morning mix down very stiff and knead for 15 minutes if possible, less will do; rub all over with lard and raise again; when light shape into loaves, raise and bake from 60 to 90 minutes, browning the first 15 minutes, then cover and bake very slowly.

MRS. J. H. WIGLE.

Rye Bread (No. 2).—Sift together 1 sifter each of rye and white flour; add three-fourths cup dry potato yeast; handful caraway seeds, if liked, and just enough water to make a very stiff dough, just as stiff as it can possibly be stirred; set at night; in the morning grease pans, stir dough well and bake in 3 small loaves in slow oven for 1 hour.

MRS. J. H. WIGLE.

Individual Loaves.—Work small pieces of dough in strands a finger long; take 3 strands for each loaf and braid; make small as possible; brush with beaten egg or sweeten water and sprinkle with poppy seeds. Allow them to raise before setting them in the oven.

MRS. BLANCHE MICHELL.

Salt Rising Bread (Tested Recipe).—Take 1 pint fresh sweet milk, 1 teaspoonful of salt, 1 pint boiling water; when milk is warm stir in flour until a thick batter, then keep in warm water until it raises to top of cup or runs over; then mix the sponge and put in pans to raise to twice the size of sponge. Bake in a moderately hot oven.

MRS. E. J. SUMNER.

Corn Bread (No. 2).—One scant cup milk; 1 egg; 1 tablespoon sugar; 1 teaspoon salt; butter size of hen's egg (melted); 1 cup flour; half cup corn meal; 1 heaping teaspoon baking powder. Stir together before putting in.

MRS. DRAKE.

Rye Bread (No. 1).—Take about two cups or one-third of sifter of white flour and other two-thirds fill with rye; into this put about 2 tablespoons of sugar, and 1 teaspoon of salt; sift these well together; then add 1 tablespoon of caraway seed; 1 cup of good potato yeast, and 2 cups of water (warm), or milk; knead well into fairly stiff dough and let rise; then work down well and roll into a narrow loaf and bake well, with a good crust. The Prineville rye flour does not require as much white flour as it's lighter than the ordinary rye.

MRS. ROSENBERG.

Corn Bread (No. 1).—One pint corn meal; one-half cup flour, pinch of salt, handful of sugar; stir into this mixture enough sour milk to make a stiff batter; melt heaping tablespoon lard and butter mixed; 1 teaspoon soda, dissolved in one-half cup boiling water; pour this with the hot melted lard of mixture, beat well and pour into greased pan and bake about 15 minutes. It may be necessary to add a little more boiling water, as mixture should be as thin as pancake batter.

FANNY R. JOHNSON.

Corn Dodgers.—To 1 quart of corn meal, add a little salt and a small tablespoon of lard; scald with boiling water, and heat lard for a few minutes; drop a large spoonful in a greased pan. The batter should be thick enough to just flatten on bottom of pan, leaving them quite high in center. Bake in a hot oven.

DIXIE.

Popovers.—One cup milk; 2 eggs, well beaten; 1 cup flour; salt to taste. Beat very thoroughly, bake in muffin rings or gem pans.

MRS. IDA MORSE.

Nut Bread.—Two cups flour; 2 teaspoons baking powder; one-half cup sugar; 1 cup sweet milk; 1 egg; sift flour, sugar and a pinch of salt together, add one-half cup chopped walnuts; beat egg and mix with milk; add this to flour; mix well; make into loaf; place in greased pan; raise 20 minutes; bake 1 hour.

DIXIE.

Boston Brown Bread.—One heaping coffee cup each of corn, rye and graham meal; sift the three kinds together as closely as possible and beat together thoroughly with one and one-half cups New Orleans or Porto Rico molasses; two cups of sweet milk; one cup sour milk; one dessert spoon soda; one teaspoon salt. When thoroughly mixed pour into a tin form or a tin pail with tight lid, place in a kettle of cold water, put on to boil as soon as mixed and keep boiling constantly for four hours. It may appear to be too thin but it is not, as this recipe was never known to fail.

MARTHA J. WIGLE.

Brown and White Sandwiches.—When baking bread, take some of the dough and mix in enough cocoa to make a good brown; then take a layer of white and a layer of the brown dough alternately; place in pan and bake as bread; slice thin and spread with butter. Delicious to serve with salad.

M. BRINK.

Breakfast Rolls.—Mix the dough in the evening, according to directions in recipe for "Bread Raised Once;" add 1 tablespoon of butter, and set where it will keep warm until morning; cut off pieces and carefully shape them into rolls, by rolling them between the hands, but do not knead them: dip in butter, set in warm place, and they will quickly rise ready for baking. These are delicious.

DIXIE.

Sweet Cream Biscuits.—Four cupfuls flour; 1 cupful cream; 1 cupful skim milk; 2 teaspoonfuls cream of tartar; 1 teaspoonful soda; 1 teaspoonful salt; sift the salt, soda and cream of tartar with the flour, and after putting the cream and milk together mix the ingredients just mentioned, handle as quickly and as little as possible and roll out without using any extra flour except a bare sprinkling on the board. Cut the biscuits half an inch thick, put in warm pans and bake in rather quick oven with good bottom heat.

H. G. D.

Coffee Rolls.—From your regular bread dough take enough to make about a quart; work into this dough a large tablespoonful of melted butter and half a cup of sugar; then knead into this mixture, one cup of dried currants which have been washed, dried, and dusted with flour; make into rolls, dip in melted butter, let them rise and bake until brown.

H. G. D.

Crumpets.—Melt one heaping tablespoon lard; add two beaten eggs and one and a half cups milk; beat three teaspoons baking powder sifted with two and a half cups flour. Crumpet rings are larger than muffin rings. Put greased rings on hot greased griddle, fill two-thirds full with batter, turn when half done.

H. G. D.

None Such Buns.—Take about 2 or 3 large cups of bread sponge when it is ready for first kneading; add 1 egg; one-half cup white sugar; butter the size of an egg. Mix all together and add sufficient flour to knead well. Let raise till light, knead and roll a little thicker than piecrust, but not as thick as for biscuit. Cut out, turn over in melted lard or butter and lard mixed; cut out another and turn in lard and put on top, thus having two layers about as thick as a biscuit. Let raise till very light. Leave plenty of room in pan, do not let buns touch. Bake in a quick oven. These buns should raise very slow and be kept away from the stove unless very cold. I set the sponge at night and in cool weather bake them for supper.

MRS. JOHN WIGLE.

Fruit Turnovers.—Make a nice, stiff paste; roll it out the usual thickness, as for pies; then cut it out into circular pieces about the size of a small tea saucer; pile the fruit on half of the paste, sprinkle over some sugar, wet the edges and turn the paste over; press the edges together, ornament them and brush with the white of an egg; sprinkle with sugar and bake on tins in a quick oven. Jam of any kind may be substituted for fresh fruits.

MRS. H. G. W.

Graham Wafers.—Four cups of graham flour, 1 cup of white flour; 1 cup of sugar; 1 cup of sweet milk; 1 cup butter, or mix with lard; 1 teaspoon of soda. Roll thin, cut with knife, dust sugar over them.

M. BRINK.

Egg Muffins (Fine).—One quart sifted flour; 3 eggs, whites and yolks beaten separately; 3 teacups of sweet milk; 1 teaspoon salt; a tablespoon of sugar; 1 large tablespoon lard or butter, and 2 heaping teaspoons baking powder. Sift together flour, sugar, salt and baking powder, rub in the lard cold, add the beaten eggs and milk, mix quickly into a smooth batter, a little thicker than for griddle cakes. Bake in well greased muffin rings or gem pans.

MRS. J. H. W.

Snails.—For one dozen and one-half snails, take 4 good cups of light bread sponge; 1 cup sugar; 2 eggs; one and one-half heaping tablespoons of butter, or butter and lard mixed. Melt butter, mix well together and knead stiff the same as for light bread. Rub lard all over it and set away to raise slowly; raise until light and puffy. Knead and roll out about half an inch thick. Spread over it melted butter, sugar, and cinnamon and dried currants. Press the currants in with rolling pin and roll all like a jelly cake and cut off about an inch thick and turn them in the lard in the pan, and set in cool place to raise. Bake quickly. Leave plenty of space around each snail for raising. When cold spread the top with powdered sugar moistened in water.

CELIA NELMS.

Dry Potato Yeast.—Take about 2 cups dry mashed potatoes; one-fourth cup sugar; add about one-half cup yeast and the least bit of water if necessary. Mix all together and let stand in warm place till light. The yeast should be as thick as mashed potatoes. It should be made fresh for each baking, saving start each time. Use yeast cakes in a little water for first start.

MRS. J. H. W.

SPECIALS

BREAKFAST DISHES

"Dinner may be pleasant,
So may social tea;
But yet, methinks the breakfast
Is the best of all the three."

Waffles.—One quart sour milk; sifted flour to make soft batter; add the well beaten yolks of 6 eggs, then the beaten whites; one-half teaspoon soda and 2 teaspoonfuls baking powder. Beat hard for a few minutes.

MRS. IDA MORSE.

Waffles.—Put into one quart sifted flour three teaspoonfuls of baking powder; one teaspoonful of salt; one of sugar, all thoroughly mixed and sifted together; add a tablespoonful of melted butter; six well beaten eggs, and a pint of sweet milk. Cook in waffle irons, heated and well greased. Serve while hot.

MRS. J. D. L.

French Toast.—Beat two eggs; add one-half cup of milk; a pinch of salt; dip into this slices of bread, and fry in hot butter to a delicate brown. Serve with butter and syrup.

Omit eggs and milk and dip bread quickly into hot salted water and fried brown makes a nice change.

MRS. C. I. WINNEK.

Minced Ham on Toast.—Chop or put through grinders bits of cold boiled or fried ham; put in pan; cover with water; add dash of red and black pepper. Cook for about 20 minutes; thicken with a little flour and add a little butter. Serve on buttered toast, moistened with a little hot water.

MRS. J. H. WIGLE.

Dried Beef Gravy.—Pick to pieces a glass of dried beef; melt a heaping tablespoon of butter in a frying pan; add beef and cook till it curls; add tablespoon or more of flour and brown; add milk, or milk and water, enough to make good gravy. Stir well and season with salt and pepper. Serve on buttered toast or on squares of light bread.

MRS. J. H. WIGLE.

Egg Hash.—Two cups chopped meat; one-half cup cold chopped ham; 1 medium sized onion chopped; 2 potatoes; 1 cup meat stock. Bake in pan until done; make hollows with spoon. Drop eggs in hollows. Put pepper, salt and small piece butter on each egg. Bake until eggs are done.

MRS. B. F. J.

Welsh Rarebit.—Take one cup of grated cheese; the yolk of one egg; one-half cup of cream; salt and cayenne pepper to taste. Toast slices of bread, butter them, plunge into hot water, place on a heated platter. Have cheese, cream and egg boiling hot, pour over toast and serve at once.

MRS. C. I. WINNEK.

Riced Eggs.—Toast and butter round pieces of bread; open a hard cooked egg lengthwise so that the white can be cut into sections like those of an orange; strain the yolk through a ricer and place on toast. Garnish the center and arrange the sections of the white to rest lengthwise against the toast. A nice white sauce may be served with this.

MRS. COLLINS ELKINS.

Egg Served in Cups.—Butter the required number of cups; break an egg or two, as desired, into each one; salt to taste, then cover and place over the fire in a pan of boiling water. Let water boil until the eggs are sufficiently cooked. Serve in same cup. Teacups will answer the place of regular poachers if one has not the poachers at hand.

L. B.

Ham Omelet.—Cut raw ham into dice; fry with butter and when cooked enough, turn the beaten eggs over it and cook as a plain omelet; if boiled ham is used mince it and mix with the eggs after they are beaten. Bacon may be used instead of ham.

MRS. H. G. D.

Baked Eggs with Bacon.—Butter a shallow baking dish; break and carefully drop into it enough eggs to form a circle; bake in a moderate oven until the whites are set, though the yolks are still soft; slice some bacon very thin and fry until crisp; take eggs from oven and garnish with the bacon.

MRS. H. G. D.

Cheese Omelet.—Beat up three eggs and add to them a tablespoon of milk and a tablespoon of grated cheese; add a little more cheese before folding; turn it out on a hot dish; grate a little cheese over it before serving.

MRS. H. G. D.

Omelet.—Beat the yolks and whites separate of 6 eggs; 4 makes a better amount to handle; add a tablespoon of water for each egg; salt and pepper and add 2 or 3 tablespoons grated cheese. Mix all together and pour into a hot iron frying pan well greased with butter. When partly done turn half over and set in oven a minute.

GRANDMA RAY.

Ham Omelet.—Place one tablespoon of butter in a hot spider; drop in six eggs; when these have remained a second add one cup of minced ham; mix together and cook until the eggs are well done.

MRS. C. I. WINNEK.

30

English Crumpets.—To one scant quart of good rich buttermilk or sour milk, add 3 or 4 well-beaten eggs; 1 teaspoon salt and same of sugar; 1 good tablespoon melted butter, if buttermilk is not used; if it is, omit the butter; flour enough to make it a little stiffer than pancake dough; about 1 teaspoon soda moistened in a little hot water, sometimes a little more or less according to the acidity of the milk. Bake like pancakes.

MRS. G. A. COVELL.

Jelly Omelet.—Make a plain omelet and just before folding together spread with some kind of jelly. Turn on a warm platter and dust it with powdered sugar.

MRS. H. G. D.

J. E. Stewart & Co.

Prineville's Leading Grocers

In making up the recipes in this book you will want the best the market affords—Spices, Extracts, Baking Powders, and in fact everything used must be first-class to insure best results. You will find in our stock the best goods and the largest assortment. For Desserts, nothing can excel our Famous Royal Club Canned Fruits.

J. E. Stewart & Co.

Prineville, Oregon

SALADS

"My salad days,
When I was green in judgment."

(To crisp celery, lettuce, cabbage and all vegetables used in salad, put in ice water for two hours before serving.)

Salad Dressing for All Salads.—Yolks of 12 eggs beaten very light; pour in slowly a large cup and a half of good vinegar; one teaspoonful of mustard, and one of salt; two tablespoons sugar; butter the size of an egg, and several dashes of both black and red pepper; beat all well together; put in double boiler and cook until thick like custard; put away in a glass jar, and when needed take out sufficient for use immediately and thin with rich cream, whipped, if possible. It will keep indefinitely before cream is added. Three or six eggs may be used by reducing the other ingredients in like proportions.

Mrs. J. H. Wigle.

Salad Dressing (No. 1).—Two eggs; one teaspoonful mustard; one-half tablespoon flour; two tablespoons sugar; one-half teaspoon salt; butter the size of an egg; one cup vinegar, diluted if very strong. Beat yolk and white separately. Mix thoroughly; put in a double boiler and cook until thickens. Just before using, thin with cream. This makes one pint and will keep.

Mrs. J. H. Crooks.

Salad Dressing (No. 2).—One egg, well beaten; one teaspoon of flour; a little salt and mustard; one-half cup of vinegar. Cook all together, stirring all the time. When cold thin with a little cream. Excellent for apple salad.

Willa Combs.

Dressing.—One-half cup vinegar; 1 cup milk (cooked); one and one-half teaspoonfuls salt; one-half teaspoonful pepper; dash cayenne pepper; three well-beaten eggs; enough sugar to sweeten, according to taste.

Frieda Lippman.

French Dressing.—Four tablespoons olive oil; one and one-half tablespoons vinegar; one-fourth teaspoon salt and white pepper; put oil in cup with opening closed; put salt and pepper in bowl, then run out half the oil; mix thoroughly; now slowly add one-half vinegar; blend; add oil and vinegar a little at a time.

X.

Sour Cream Dressing.—One-half cup of good rich cream, beaten light; add one-half cup vinegar, pinch of salt and pepper to taste. The above is good for lettuce or cabbage.

MRS. G. A. COVELL.

Hot Dressing for Lettuce.—Fry the grease from a slice of bacon; add one-half cup good vinegar; salt and pepper, and pour over lettuce while hot; a small onion may be added to the bacon and cooked until tender, which makes a good change.

MRS. MARY E. WHITE.

Dressing for Hot Slaw.—One egg beaten light; a little mustard, salt, pepper, and sugar; about one-fourth spoonful of each, except the pepper; one-half cup of vinegar. Cook until thick and add chopped cabbage and cook until well heated.

MRS. J. H. WIGLE.

Waldorf Salad (No. 1).—Two bunches celery, cut fine; twice as many sliced chopped apples; one pound chopped walnuts.

L. B.

Waldorf Salad (No. 2)—Known as Celery and Apple Salad).—Three or four tart apples peeled and quartered; these cut into small bits; a bunch of celery cut into small bits; a cup of walnut meats broken. Toss all together and mix well with salad dressing. The apple and celery must be cut and not chopped, and do not let it stand, for it is apt to turn dark.

MRS. J. H. WIGLE.

New Salad.—Prepare one package of lemon Jell-O according to directions. When it begins to congeal, add one heaping cup of English walnuts, stuffed olives and pickles cut in small pieces. Put in small molds. When ready to use, turn out on shredded lettuce and serve with mayonnaise.

MRS. LOUIS DOONAR.

Fruit Salad.—Equal parts of orange and sliced pineapple cut into bits; one-half cup cherries; one cup chopped nuts; one-half cup cocoanut.

MRS. J. N. WILLIAMSON.

Fruit Salad.—One teacup of Malaga grapes; one teacup English walnuts; one teacup celery cut in short pieces; three oranges; three bananas. Seed the Malaga grapes and set on ice while preparing the rest. Chop walnuts; cut the celery in short pieces; peel oranges; slice and remove seeds; peel bananas and cut in thin, crosswise slices. Line a salad bowl with crisp, tender lettuce leaves; mix all the ingredients, tossing them up lightly; squeeze over this the juice of a lemon and heap with mayonnaise dressing.

BERTHA BALDWIN.

Pear Salad.—Use one-half large cooked pear for each person; remove the juice and sprinkle generously with chopped English walnuts. Serve on lettuce leaves with mayonnaise dressing.

MRS. J. E. RYAN.

Apple Salad.—Core, but do not peel, six ripe apples; scoop them out a little; fill them with cold, cooked chicken minced fine and mixed with finely minced green pepper; a little salt and just enough cream to moisten the chicken. Now put these apples in a steamer and cook them until almost tender, but not in the least soft. When cool put them on ice until very cold, then serve each one on a bed of lettuce and pile plenty of mayonnaise dressing around and on the top of each.

BERTHA BALDWIN.

Cherry Salad (No. 1).—Stone about a half pound of cherries; sprinkle with sugar and put then into a wire basket to drain; peel and dice a small cucumber, salt and put it on ice for several hours; blanch and chop a half pound of almonds; wash and drain the cucumber mix it with the cherries, add the almonds and cover with a whipped cream dressing. Serve ice cold on crisp lettuce leaves.

BERTHA BALDWIN.

Cherry Salad (No. 2).—For this salad one quart of ox heart cherries are carefully stoned, and the cavities filled with nuts. Serve in lettuce cups or little salad baskets. Garnish with white mayonnaise.

BERTHA BALDWIN.

Peach Salad.—Peel and slice six large peaches; one-half cup almonds blanched and chopped fine; four peach kernels. Make salad dressing as given and mix the whole together. Serve on crisp lettuce leaves with whipped cream.

FRIEDA LIPPMAN.

Banana Salad (No. 1).—Peel and slice a banana lengthwise; lay it on a lettuce leaf and pour over it salad dressing and sprinkle chopped walnuts over it.

MRS. BABBIDGE.

Banana Salad (No. 2).—Cut up fine two or three bananas and two or three apples and a bunch of celery; add cup of walnuts, or pecans preferred; mix with salad dressing. This is excellent. It makes a nice change to serve in banana skins on lettuce leaves.

CELIA NELMS.

Potato Salad (No. 1).—Boil potatoes in their jackets; peel and salt while warm; chop or slice and to six large potatoes use a good sized onion, chopped; two hard boiled eggs, and a little parsley. Pour salad dressing over while potatoes are warm and set away to cool. Should stand three or four hours.

MRS. ALBERT RAY.

Macaroni Salad.—One cup of cooked macaroni; six hard boiled eggs; one-half cup chopped olives; three tablespoons of onions, chopped, and one cup of celery cut up. Mix all together with good dressing.

MRS. ROSENBERG.

Cabbage Salad (No. 1).—If the cabbage is not crisp let it stand in cold water several hours before using. Chop fine and mix with salad dressing, or with a little sugar, salt, pepper and vinegar.

FANNY R. JOHNSON.

Potato Salad (No. 2).—One and one-half cups cold potatoes cut in cubes; small bunch chives cut fine; three hard boiled eggs, sliced. Mix thoroughly with mayonnaise dressing. Cover platter with crisp lettuce leaves, spread salad on top. This looks nice to put sliced eggs on top.

Mrs. B. F. J.

Lettuce Dressing.—Pour over the lettuce two-thirds cup cream; one-half cup of sugar; mix a dressing of two eggs, two tablespoonfuls of sugar, one cup vinegar, salt and pepper. Cook until it comes to a boil, let cool before pouring on the lettuce.

Mrs. C. J. Johnson.

Cabbage Salad (No. 2).—One small head of cabbage, chopped fine; salt and pepper to taste; dressing, one-half cup of vinegar, two eggs well beaten, one tablespoon of sugar, butter size of walnut, or one teaspoonful of olive oil, one-half teaspoonful of mustard. Stir while cooking and boil until thick. Let cool and pour over cabbage.

Mrs. Dobbs.

Cabbage and Apple Salad.—Crisp the cabbage by standing in cold water; add two or three tart apples and mix well with dressing.

Mrs. Maupin.

Tomato Salad.—Slice tomatoes one-half inch thick; put in a frying basket, sprinkle with salt and celery salt and stand on ice. When ready to serve place on the slices hard boiled eggs chopped and mixed with cream cheese; over this put a mayonnaise or whipped cream dressing. Serve on a lettuce leaf. This makes a pretty individual salad.

Mrs. Collins W. Elkins.

Pea Salad.—Soften one tablespoon of gelatine in cold water and add it to half cup of hot, highly seasoned stock; strain and cool; when beginning to set, stir in lightly one-half cup cooked fresh peas; mould in small cups. Serve with dressing and garnish with celery top or parsley.

Mrs. Collins W. Elkins.

Asparagus Salad.—Cut tender tips, drop into boiling water and cook ten minutes; drain and place on ice. When ready to serve, place on tender lettuce leaves and use a dressing. Serve with crackers, cream cheese and olives.

Mrs. Collins W. Elkins.

Lettuce and Potato Salad.—Mix cold mashed potatoes with a little salad dressing; make a nest of lettuce leaves, head lettuce preferred, on a platter; put potatoes in the center and pour a salad dressing over lettuce leaves.

Mrs. J. H. Wigle.

Chicken Salad.—Boil a chicken down until but little liquor is left; season well; tear meat from bones in small pieces; take an equal amount of celery chopped fine or cut into bits; two or three hard boiled eggs, chopped. Mix all together and use a generous amount of salad dressing. This amount will serve about a dozen.

Mrs. J. H. Wigle.

36

Chicken Salad.—Stew a chicken in as little water as possible; when done remove the skin and set away to cool; remove bones and select the white part; cut into dice the size of a hazlenut or finer; three stalks of celery cut fine; whites of ten eggs, hard boiled, cut in half rings; pour over this a rich mayonnaise dressing made as follows: stir together 2 tablespoons sugar, 1 teaspoon dry mustard, 1 tablespoon celery salt and a dash of cayenne pepper; add 1 small cup vinegar; beat yolks of 6 eggs and pour slowly into vinegar, beating all the time to prevent curdling; then add one cup of cream and put over the fire, and whip with egg spoon until it thickens; remove at once and do not let it boil; whip till cold and if too thick thin with cream; stir lightly with silver fork after it is poured over the chicken.   Mrs. J. E. Ryan.

Emergency Salad.—Two or three cold boiled potatoes; one hard boiled egg; a small onion; a pickle and a little parsley and bits of cold meat loaf, hash, or fowl all cut into dice or chopped and mixed with salad dressing, makes a good dish of left overs and helps out a supper or luncheon.   Mrs. J. H. Wigle.

Summer Salad.—A few stalks of celery cut fine; a green pepper shredded; a few tomatoes sliced. Mix this with salad dressing and lay on lettuce leaves. Makes a delicious salad with cold meats.
          Mrs. Zimmerman.

Lobster Salad.—One can lobster; one head celery; one cupful chopped cabbage; six hard boiled eggs; salt and pepper to taste. Serve with French dressing.   Mrs. I. Morse.

Cove Oyster Salad.—Snip up the oysters from a small can; pour the juice over three or four small crackers broken into small pieces; add oysters to crackers; a cupful of walnut meats broken a little; three or four hard boiled eggs chopped; a large bunch of celery chopped; toss all together lightly and mix well with salad dressing. Cabbage may be used with celery salt in place of celery.
          Mrs. Lafferty.

Sardine Salad.—A few cold boiled potatoes chopped; a can of sardines with oil rinsed off and minced fine; three or four small sour pickles chopped. Mix all with salad dressing.
          Mrs. J. H. Wigle.

Salmon Salad (No. 1).—Cold boiled or baked salmon, minced, with a little lemon juice poured over it; use twice as much cold potato chopped fine and mixed with salad dressing. Canned salmon may be used but be sure to pour boiling water over salmon to take off the oil, and cool before using.   Mrs. J. H. Wigle.

Salmon Salad (No. 2).—Put a can of salmon in a kettle of hot water; let boil 20 minutes; remove the top and drain off the oil; place salmon in a dish and cover with cold vinegar. Dressing—beat the yolks of 2 raw eggs with the yolks of 2 hard boiled eggs, as fine as possible; add gradually 1 tablespoon of mustard, 3 tablespoons melted butter, a little salt, pepper and vinegar to taste; beat the mixture thoroughly, then cover a platter with crisp lettuce leaves (if you have the good fortune to have the lettuce), then put the salmon on it and pour dressing over it.   Carrie D. Rice.

MISCELLANEOUS

"Would you know how first he met her?
She was cutting bread and butter."

Fruit Punch (No. 1).—Peel 6 oranges; take the juice of 4 and 2 cut in thin slices or small pieces; 1 can sliced pineapple; 1 dozen lemons; 1 pint sugar; 1 quart water; 1 pint strong tea. Make syrup of the sugar and water, when cold add 1 bottle strawberry syrup and 2 gallons water; cut the pineapple in dice; it improves it to add 1 bottle of apollinaris water. Serve very cold.

I. M.

Fruit Punch (No. 2).—Dissolve about 1 teaspoonful citric acid crystals in half glass water; roll and squeeze the juice from 1 dozen lemons and 3 oranges; add acid and about 1 quart fruit juice is good, but combination of several is better; peach, strawberry and pineapple make a delightful combination or preserved cherries, currant jam or jelly is the old rule for mince meat, a little of everything and plenty of it is applicable to this; add water enough to make about 3 gallons and sweeten to taste. When ready to serve add 1 or 2 oranges sliced. One must use their own judgment in using acid and sugar.

Mrs. J. H. W.

Cheese Straws.—Take nice rich pie crust, roll out about as thin as for pie; cover with grated cheese; add a little red pepper; fold over edges two or three times and roll thin again; add more cheese and double edges and roll thin again. Repeat this until no more cheese can be added; roll about as thin as for pie and cut into strips an inch wide and about four inches long and bake until light brown.

Mrs. J. H. Wigle.

Grandma Bell's Coffee.—Pure Java and Mocha mixed, allowing a tablespoon to each person and one for the pot. Mix with beaten egg and moisten with warm water; then pour over boiling water, a good cup for each person, and boil ten minutes. Let stand a few minutes before serving.

Cream Puffs.—One-half cup butter melted in one cup of hot water; put in a small tin pan on the stove to boil; while boiling stir in one cup of flour; take off and let cool; when cool stir in three eggs, one at a time, without beating; beat thoroughly; drop on buttered tins and bake in a hot oven thirty minutes. Filling: one cup of milk, one egg, one-half cup sugar, thicken with corn starch and flavor with vanilla.

Martha J. Wigle.

Egg Farci.—Cut "hard-boiled" eggs in halves, crosswise; remove yolks, and put whites aside in pairs; mash yolks, and add equal amount of cold cooked chicken or veal, finely chopped; moisten with melted butter or mayonnaise. Season to taste with salt, pepper, lemon juice, mustard and cayenne. Shape and refill whites.

LORENE WINNEK.

Sandwich Filling—Sardine.—One can sardines, rinsed with hot water to remove oil; scrape off skin; chop; squeeze a little lemon juice over them and mix with salad dressings. **Cheese.**—Mashed or grated and mixed with mustard and red pepper. **Egg.**—Boil eggs hard; chop; mix with salad dressing and salt and pepper, or mix with cream and a little dry mustard, salt and pepper. **Fig.**—Put figs through grinder; mix with cream, or dates and figs mixed. **Ham.**—Grind cold boiled ham; mix with mustard and cream or salad dressing. **Mock Chicken.**—Grind veal and the tenderloin of pork boiled tender and seasoned with salt, pepper and a little mustard moistened with cream. **Lettuce or Peppergrass** mixed with salad dressing and a little ham or cold meat of any kind chopped makes a good filling if used at once.

COMMITTEE.

Strawberry Shortcake.—One pint flour; pinch of salt; one teaspoonful baking powder sifted together; heaping tablespoonful of lard or butter or the two mixed, rubbed well with the flour; add milk enough to make a stiff dough; handle as little and as quickly as possible; roll out about one-quarter inch thick; cut with biscuit cutter; turn over in melted lard or butter; put another one on top and bake a light brown in a quick oven. When done they will fall apart. Mash strawberries, sweeten and put between and on top. Other fruit may be substituted and it may be baked in two large sheets, but the individual ones serve much daintier and saves cutting the warm cake.

MRS. J. H. W.

SPECIALS

SPECIALS

PIES AND PASTRY

"No soil upon earth is so dear to our eyes
As the soil we first stirred in terrestrial pies."

Apple Pie.—Take 4 large tart apples, peel and slice finely; to make pie paste take a cup and a half of flour; add to this a pinch of salt and a pinch of baking powder and two tablespoonfuls of lard with enough cold water to moisten the dough; line a pie pan with the paste, put in apples, add sugar to suit; sprinkle with cinnamon and bits of butter. This makes a very good pie.

MRS. H. G. D.

Mock Lemon Pie.—Two cups of sugar; one teaspoonful citric acid, dissolved in two cups of boiling water; two and one-half tablespoonfuls of starch or flour; four eggs. This makes two pies.

MRS. ANGIE SMITH.

Halved Apple Pie.—Pare and cut in half tart apples; bellfleurs are best; remove cores and place in rich crust, cut side up; allow cup of sugar and tablespoon of butter to each pie, strewing sugar over, butter cut in bits. Bake in one crust. Serve with cream. Rich and delicious.

DIXIE LAND.

Apple Custard Pie.—Peel, core and stew sour apples; then mash very fine. For each pie allow yolk of one egg; one cup of sugar; one-fourth cup of butter; one-fourth nutmeg. Bake in lower crust. Beat whites of eggs for top as usual way.

MRS. C. A. RIDDLE.

Custard Pie (No. 1).—One-half cup sugar; one quart rich milk; two tablespoonfuls corn starch; yolks of four eggs. Put on stove and stir until thick. Beat whites of four eggs to stiff froth, add two tablespoonfuls sugar, spread on top, and brown. This will make two pies.

MRS. W. A. B.

Custard Pie (No. 2).—Three eggs; one-half cup of sugar; a pinch of salt; one teaspoon of vanilla; one pint of milk. Beat eggs and sugar together, stir in other ingredients well, beat whites of one egg for filling and two for frosting. Bake on bottom crust.

MRS. C. A. RIDDLE.

Cream Pie (No. 2).—One pint milk; yolks two eggs, beaten; three teaspoons flour; one-half cup sugar. Put milk and sugar on to boil; when boiling add eggs with a little milk and then cook until it thickens.

L. B.

Sliced Apple Pie (Tested Recipe).—Line a pie plate with rich pastry and fill with sliced tart apples; sprinkle two heaping table-spoonfuls of sugar and grate a little nutmeg over the apples; cover with a sheet of pastry with openings cut for escape of steam. Wet the edges of under crust before putting on the upper and then pinch the two edges together.

MRS. E. J. SUMNER.

Aunt Almeda's Cream Pie.—One pint of milk on stove, part cream if have it; three eggs yolks; one tablespoon of flour; three tablespoons of sugar, scant. Beat well with spoon, pour into hot milk and add lump of butter. Beat with spoon, cook this until thick, flavor with vanilla. Have crust baked; when cool add cream to crust and beat whites of eggs, four tablespoons of sugar, one teaspoon lemon juice, and flavor with vanilla. Set in oven to brown.

MRS. A. THOMSON.

Cream Pie (No. 1).—One and one-half cups thick cream, scant cups; sugar; two tablespoonfuls flour; whites two eggs; flavor with nutmeg; mix cream and sugar; let stand about 15 minutes, so sugar will be thoroughly dissolved; beat whites of eggs to stiff froth, add last. Line pan with paste, bake, then put in cream. Bake very slow until cream thickens.

M. ROWAN.

Cocoanut Pie.—One-half cup prepared cocoanut, soaked 5 minutes in two cups of milk; one cup sugar; two eggs; butter the size of a walnut; one tablespoon cornstarch. Put the milk and cocoanut over the stove in a double boiler; when hot stir in sugar, butter and yolk of the eggs, and cornstarch mixed with a little cold milk. Cook and pour in pie shell previously baked. Spread well beaten whites (with four tablespoonfuls sugar) on top and brown.

Lemon Pie.—One cup of boiling water; one cup of sugar; one tablespoon of cornstarch. Boil together. Grate rind of one lemon, also juice; three eggs; save one white for top of pie. Line plate with paste, add sugar and water to eggs and lemon, pour into lined plate and bake.

MRS. CASSIE B. HEATH.

Orange Pie (Tested Recipe).—The juice and grated rind of two oranges, four eggs, four tablespoons of sugar, one tablespoonful of butter. Cream the butter and sugar, add the beaten yolks of the eggs, then the oranges, and lastly the whites, beaten to a froth and mixed in lightly. Bake with an under crust only.

MRS. E. J. SUMNER.

Orange Pie.—Grate the rind of one and use the juice of two large oranges; stir together a large cupful of sugar, a heaping tablespoonful flour; add to this the well-beaten yolks of three eggs; two tablespoons of melted butter; reserve the whites for frosting. Turn this into a pie-pan lined with pie paste and bake in a quick oven. When done so as to resemble a finely baked custard, spread on top the whites of the eggs, beaten with two tablespoons sugar. Return to the oven to brown slightly.

MRS. J. H. HAUER.

Pumpkin Pie (No. 1).—One cup canned pumpkin; one-third cup sugar; one-half teaspoon salt; one-fourth teaspoon cinnamon, ginger and nutmeg; two eggs; one cup rich cream; mix sugar, salt and spice, add pumpkin and eggs, beat slightly, and add milk. Bake in one crust. After pie has baked and cold, cover top with one and one-half cups of whipped cream sweetened and flavored.

MRS. HARRY LANIUS.

Pumpkin Pie (No. 2).—Two eggs; one and one-half cups of sugar; one pint of milk; one pint strained pumpkin; one-half teaspoon of ginger; one teaspoon of cinnamon; one tablespoon molasses. This is for two pies.

MRS. C. A. RIDDLE.

Rhubarb Lemon Pie (Tested Recipe).—For each pie, one cup stewed rhubarb; yolks of four eggs, well beat; one cup sugar; two tablespoonfuls of flour; two teaspoonfuls of lemon. Bake in one crust. When done frost with the whites of eggs and bake until brown.

MABEL WINDOM.

Carrot Pie.—Grate one-half cupful of sweet raw carrots; one-half cupful sugar; three eggs, beat together; then put in a cup of cream. Bake with one crust.

MRS. C. C. BABBIDGE.

Sweet Potato Pie.—Peel and slice thin 4 large sweet potatoes; boil until tender; make a rich crust, line a deep pan with crust, then place layer of potatoes and crust alternately, using plenty of sugar and butter size of an egg; pour hot water over all and bake for twenty minutes; take from oven and put crust over all and bake slowly until well done.

S. D.

Mamma's Vinegar Pie (No. 1).—One cup each of hot water, good vinegar, and of sugar; place on the stove and heat to near boiling; add 2 well beaten eggs, and 2 tablespoonfuls of cornstarch, dissolved in a little cold water; a piece of butter size of an egg. When thick flavor with lemon. Have crust baked, put in filling and frost. This will make two pies.

MRS. T. Y. SUMNER.

Vinegar Pie (No. 2).—Two cups sugar; one-half cup syrup; 1 cup water; one-half cup vinegar; 2 tablespoons cornstarch; 4 eggs; butter size of walnut. This makes two pies.

L. B.

PUDDINGS AND DUMPLINGS

"Love in a cottage and cottage pudding with it."

Apple Dumpling Baked.—For 4 dumplings: Sift 1 pint flour, 1 teaspoonful baking powder and a pinch of salt; 1 heaping tablespoonful lard or butter, rubbed well with flour; enough milk to make stiff dough; pinch off piece and roll out round; place an apple, peeled, cored and halved in center, the two halves put together with a little butter in center; sprinkle with cinnamon; pull up the dough and pinch it all together; moisten with water if necessary; place in pan so that they exactly fit, they will keep shape better; put a cup of sugar over them and enough water to half cover; put lid over them till last few minutes. Bake till apples are tender.

MARTHA J. WIGLE.

Apple Pudding (No. 1).—One cup of sifted flour; one teaspoon of baking powder; one cup milk; one tablespoonful of butter; one cup sugar; one egg; slice apples and put between the batter with a little cinnamon over the apples, also a little salt, and bake in moderate oven. Sauce: One teaspoon of cornstarch blended with milk, then pour it into a cup of boiling milk, add sugar and piece of butter; let boil a few minutes; add one teaspoon vanilla.

MRS. BLANCHE MICHEL.

Apple Pudding (No. 2).—Stew half dozen apples in half pint milk; make a batter of two eggs; a piece of butter size of an egg; 1 teaspoonof baking powder; flour to make thin batter; pour over apples and bake.

LIBBIE COMBS.

Plum Pudding, Baked.—Two pounds flour; 1 pound currants; 1 pound raisins; 1 pound suet; 2 eggs; 1 pint milk; a few slices of candied peel; chop suet and mix fruit and suet with the flour; moisten with the eggs, well beaten, and add sufficient milk to make of the pudding a good thick batter; put in buttered dish and bake in a good oven about two and one-half hours. Serve with sauce.

MRS. JACK SUMNER.

Baked Suet Pudding.—To one-half cup chopped suet, add 2 cupfuls bread crumbs; one-half cup sugar; one-half pound seeded raisins; 2 well beaten eggs, and one scant cupful flour, sifted with one teaspoonful baking powder; place in a buttered baking dish and pour over cold milk enough to almost cover. Bake about 30 minutes or a little longer. Serve hot with whipped cream or any other preferred sauce.

MRS. T. Y. SUMNER

Suet Pudding.—One cupful of suet, chopped fine; 1 cupful of N. O. L. molasses; 1 cupful of sour milk; 1 teaspoon soda in sour milk; three and one-half cupfuls sifted flour; 1 teaspoon cinnamon, cloves, nutmegs, a little salt. Boil three hours in pudding mold. Set in a kettle of water. Eat with white sauce or whipped cream.

MRS. J. H. HAUER.

Suet Pudding.—One cup each of chopped suet, raisins, molasses, and milk; one egg; three cups of sifted flour; a little salt and one-half teaspoon of soda. Steam three hours. Serve with sweet sauce. Be sure to put a cloth over the steamer.

Sauce.—Rub one tablespoonful of butter into a cup of sugar; add two beaten eggs and work all to a froth. Wet one-half a teaspoonful cornstarch and stir into the mixture; then stir in five tablespoonfuls of boiling milk, beating well all the time. Set the dish in a pan of boiling water and simmer five minutes. Flavor with lemon.

JENNIE D. PICKETT.

Chocolate Puddng.—Put 1 quart of milk on to heat in double boiler with a bar of grated chocolate or about 2 tablespoons cocoa or ground chocolate; mix a small cup of sugar with one-half cup flour and add to milk when hot; cook till it is thick; flavor well with vanilla and beat into mixture the whites of 2 well beaten eggs. Put away to cool and serve with cream. It may be necessary to add a little more flour stirred smooth in water to thicken.

MRS. J. H. W.

Tapioca Pudding.—Soak one cup of tapioca in new milk over night; add one quart of milk; a lump of butter; a little salt, and boil; beat the yolks of four eggs with one cup of sugar; then add one cup of cocoanut. Cook till very thick. Beat whites of eggs; add three tablespoons of sugar; one of vanilla; place on top, brown and serve when cold.

EMMA EDWARDS.

Old English Plum Pudding.—One pound each raisins seeded; currants, and suet chopped fine; 1 pound bread crumbs, one-half pound sugar; one and one-half ounces preserved or candied lemon, or citron; one-half nutmeg grated; 1 teaspoon mace; one-half dozen eggs, well beaten. Work all thoroughly together, tie in floured cloth or buttered bucket with lid and boil not less than 5 hours, and 10 hours improves the flavor of the pudding, but it must not stop boiling.

Sauce.—Cream together one-half cup butter; one-half cup sugar, into which beat the yolk of 1 egg; add 1 pint hot milk. Just before serving add beaten white of egg and flavor to taste.

SELECTED.

Woodford Pudding.—Three eggs; one-half cup of sugar; one-half cup of butter; one cup of flour; one cup of preserves or jam; one teaspoon of soda, dissolved in six teaspoonfuls of sour milk; spices to taste. Mix and steam three hours. Serve with any good pudding sauce.

MRS. E. V. WINNEK.

Mystery Pudding.—Peel some nice tart apples, quarter and slice layer into a baking dish; cut up any pieces of dried cake, cookies, or ginger bread you have on hand, several different kinds are best; add a little butter, cinnamon and sugar, then another layer of apples and one of cake, having apples on top; add sugar, butter and cinnamon, and pour over all a little water; if cake is very dry and apples not juicy use more; cover and bake till apples are tender. Just before they are done remove, cover and brown. Serve with cream, or the following sauce: One cup sugar; heaping tablespoonful flour; enough boiling water to make like thin gravy; cook 5 minutes, and add lump of butter size large walnut and teaspoon vanilla. This sauce is good for almost all puddings by adding a little more butter. Mrs. J. H.

Chocolate Bread Pudding.—One and one-half squares of chocolate melted in a little milk; 1 quart of milk; 1 cup of bread crumbs soaked in milk; beat 2 eggs with 1 cup of light brown sugar; mix all together and flavor with vanilla. Bake in buttered dish in slow oven till like custard. Mrs. C. S. Edwards.

Marshmallow Pudding.—A heaping tablespoon of gelatine, soaked in cold water; then dissolve in 1 cup of hot water; beat gradually into well beaten whites of four eggs; add 1 cup of sugar and beat for 20 or 30 minutes; divide into 3 parts and color 1 part pink and use for the middle layer; fruit or nuts may be used in the two white layers. Serve with whipped cream. Hazel Lannies.

John's Delight.—Two cups of bread crumbs: half cup of chopped suet or butter; one-half cup of molasses: one egg; one cup raisins; one cup of sweet milk, with half a teaspoonful of soda dissolved in it; one-half teaspoonful of cloves; one of cinnamon, and a pinch of salt. Steam two hours in a pudding boiler. Serve with foaming sauce. Mrs. C. I. Winnek.

Endorsed by the Foremost
European Authorities

THOMPSON THE INTERNATIONALLY INDORSED **SIGHT EXPERT**

CORBETT BLD'G. SECOND FLOOR 5TH & MORRISON **PORTLAND, ORE**

Thompson's ability has been recognized by the highest authorities in Europe. Moree, Germany's foremost physician, May 16, 1908, says:

"The rapidity and accuracy with which Thompson corrects eye trouble is nothing short of marvelous."

The London Daily Mail;
The New York Times;
The Chicago Tribune;
    May 14, '08, says:
"R. A. Thompson, an American optician. was called upon while in Berlin to deliver several lectures on the eye to students of both German and American nationality. Eminent German authorities have declared his system of eye testing a great aid to science."

The British Optician, London, May 29, '08, says:
"By the Thompson system of fitting glasses a mistake is impossible."

The London Science Siftings (the Scientific American of Europe). June 6, '08, says:
"A number of prominent oculists were greatly astonished last evening at the remarkable skill of R. A. Thompson, an American optician."

Le Figaro, Paris, June 16, '08, says:
"R. A. Thompson, an American optician, astonished the medical world last evening with an important discovery for sight testing."

IF YOU NEED GLASSES THOMPSON CAN FIT YOU
ONE CHARGE
COVERS ENTIRE COST OF EXAMINATION,
GLASSES, FRAMES

COOKIES & DOUGHTNUTS

"I was more than stewed in grease like a Dutch dish."

Doughnuts.—One cup new milk; one cup sugar; two eggs; salt; two teaspoons baking powder; flour to mix very soft.

MRS. CARRIE D. RICE.

Doughnuts.—One cup of sugar; 3 eggs: 2 tablespoons of butter, melted; 4 cups of flour; 3 teaspoons baking powder; 1 cup of milk.

MRS. A. THOMSON.

Doughnuts.—One cup sugar; 2 eggs; 1 cup cream (sweet), not too rich; flour enough for soft dough; 1 teaspoonful baking powder. Nutmeg or any other.

MRS. THOMAS BRINT.

Doughnuts.—One cup sugar: two eggs: one cup sour milk: one teaspoon soda; three tablespoons melted lard. Flavor with nutmeg.

N. DUDLEY.

Doughnuts.—Boil 3 large potatoes; when done. mash fine and strain through colander; while still hot add 1 large tablespoon of butter; 2 cups of sugar; and 2 cups of sweet milk; 3 eggs; flour enough to roll with 4 teaspoons of baking powder; salt; pepper, and nutmeg. This recipe will make about five dozen.

MRS. B. F. J.

Doughnuts.—Three eggs; one and one-half cups sugar; 1 cup of buttermilk; 1 teaspoon soda; 4 tablespoons melted butter; teaspoon nutmeg; salt. Mix stiff with flour, fry in hot grease and roll in sugar. Fine.

BEATRICE JOHNSON.

Ginger Snaps.—One cup molasses; one cup sugar; one cup butter and lard mixed; one egg; one-half cup boiling water; one teaspoonful soda dissolved in water; two teaspoonfuls ginger; flour enough to mold rather soft.

MRS. CARRIE D. RICE.

Ginger Snaps.—Two cups molasses; 1 cup sugar; 1 cup melted butter or shortening; let the above come to a boil, then add 2 teaspoons soda; 1 quart flour; 1 teaspoon ginger; 1 teaspoon cinnamon; one-fourth teaspoon cloves; one-half teaspoon allspice; 1 teaspoon salt. Dissolve the soda and pour it into the molasses; pour boiled molasses, sugar and shortening into flour. Roll very thin.

MRS. ALEX BOUICK.

51

Ginger Cookies.—One cup sugar; two cups molasses; one cup lard; two teaspoonfuls ginger; two teaspoonfuls soda dissolved in two-thirds cup of cold water; flour to mold soft.　　Mrs. Isom Cleek.

Ginger Cake.—Four cups flour; 1 cup butter; 2 cups sugar; 1 cup molasses; 1 cup sour milk; 4 eggs, beaten separately; 1 tablespoonful ginger; cloves; cinnamon; 1 teaspoon soda; add whites last.
　　Mrs. W. F. King.

Gingerbread Sponge.—Beat together 1 egg and 1 cupful brown sugar; add one-half teaspoonful cloves; 1 teaspoonful each ginger and cinnamon; one-half teaspoonful salt; sift 1 teaspoonful soda into one-half cup of molasses; add to first mixture; beat in alternately 1½ cupfuls sifted flour and one-half cupful hot water. Pour into shallow pans and bake 20 minutes.　　E. True Shattuck.

Soft Ginger Bread.—One cup brown sugar; 1 cup New Orleans molasses; one-third cup shortening; 1 tablespoon vinegar; 1 tablespoon ginger; 2 teaspoons soda; 1 cup boiling water.
　　N. Dudley.

Hobson's Gingerbread.—One-half cup brown sugar poured over 1 egg; one-half cup black molasses; 1 rounded teaspoon soda beaten in molasses; three-fourths cup hot water; 1 teaspoon cinnamon; 1 teaspoon ginger; 1 large tablespoon melted butter; about one and one-half cups flour. Thinner batter than cake. Bake in slow oven. A handful chopped nuts added last are fine.　　Mrs. C. S. Edwards.

Cookies.—Two cups of sugar; 1 cup of butter; 1 cup of sour cream; 3 eggs; 1 teaspoon soda.　　Libbie Combs.

Auntie May's Cookies.—One pound butter; 2 cups white sugar; 6 eggs; 2 teaspoons baking powder; flour enough to roll; vanilla flavoring; cream, butter and sugar; add eggs beaten light; then flavoring and flour; roll very thin, place in pan, brush each one with a rag dipped in cream or milk, sprinkle a little sugar and cinnamon, and bake a light brown. Have been known to keep a year and better then than when first baked.

Drop Cookies.—One cup shortening; 1 cup sugar; 3 eggs; two-thirds cup sour milk; one-half teaspoon soda; 2 cups flour; 2 cups wheat flakes; 1 cup chopped raisins, nuts, figs or mixture of each; one-half teaspoon cinnamon. Drop from spoon on greased tins.
　　E. True Shattuck.

Fruit Cookies.—One and one-half cups brown sugar; 1 cup butter; 3 eggs; 1 cup chopped raisins; 2 tablespoonfuls sweet milk; 1 teaspoonful soda, dissolved in milk; 1 teaspoonful cinnamon; flour sufficient to handle.　　Mrs. L. B True.

Rolled Oat Cookies.—One cup brown sugar; one-half cup butter; one-half cup lard; one cup flour; two eggs; two teaspoonfuls baking powder; two and one-half cups violet oats; salt; cinnamon or nutmeg. Melt butter and lard, mix sugar and eggs, then add flour and oats, drop in well greased pans, and bake in hot oven.
　　Mrs. Carrie D. Rice.

Rolled Oat Cookies.—One cup butter; 1 cup lard; 2 cups sugar; one-half cup sweet milk; four and one-half cups flour; 4 cups rolled oats; 3 eggs; 1 pound raisins; one-half teaspoon soda in a little water; one-half teaspoon salt; 1 tablespoon allspice; 1 tablespoon cinnamon; 1 teaspoon baking powder. The way to bake the oat meal cookies: The dough must be worked with the hands and will be very stiff; use well greased pans, and with a fork lift out a lump of the dough and flatten it down with a knife, leaving an inch space between. Bake in a moderate oven. Your pan will be full.

Mrs. S. J. Newson.

Oat Meal Rocks.—One cup shortening; 1 cup sugar; 2 eggs; 4 tablespoons sour milk; 1 scant teaspoon soda; 1 cup raisins mashed in nut grinder; 1 teaspoon cinnamon; 1 cup white flour; three and three-fourths cups oat meal. Drop by teaspoonful on buttered tins. These are delicious.

Ollie Elkins Stewart.

53

CAKES AND CAKE FILLING

"With weights and measures just and true,
Oven of even heat;
Well buttered tins and quiet nerves,
Success will be complete."

Angel Fig Cake.—Sift together 4 times one and one-half cups sugar; one cup flour; one teaspoonful cream tartar; stir in this very lightly whites of eleven eggs thoroughly beaten; flavor with one-half teaspoon lemon extract. Bake fifty minutes in a slow oven, not opening the oven for thirty minutes. Turn pan over on a rack and let cake remain in pan one hour; cover with soft frosting flavored with lemon. Decorate with chopped figs. This is very good.   MRS. H. G. D.

Bride's Cake.—Three cups of sugar; 1 cup butter; 1 of sweet milk; 3 cups of flour; 1 cup cornstarch; 1 heaping teaspoon of baking powder. Sift the flour, sugar and yeast powder several times, then cream with butter. The last thing add the whites of 12 eggs well beaten. This is a large cake and one-half of the above will make an average cake. Use only a level teaspoon of baking powder if one-half of the amount is used. Add flavoring.   MRS. ROSENBERG.

Brown Cake.—One and one-half cups sugar; one-half cup molasses; 3 eggs; three-fourths cup butter; 1 cup raisins; 1 cup sour milk; 1 teaspoon soda; 1 of cinnamon; a pinch of salt; one-half teaspoon cloves; 1 teaspoon allspice; 4 cups flour. Bake one hour.
    MRS. J. H. HAUER.

Potato Cake.—Two cups white sugar; 1 cup butter; 1 teaspoon cinnamon, cloves and nutmeg; 1 cup mashed potatoes; 4 eggs; one-half cup milk; 1 cup nuts and 1 of raisins; 2 cups flour; 2 teaspoons baking powder; 1 cup chocolate.   MRS. J. H. HAUER.

Black Cake (Very Nice).—One-half cup water; 1 cup sugar; one-half large cake chocolate, cooked till the chocolate is melted; add yolk of one egg and cook till thick. When cool add following cake batter: One-half cup butter; one cup sugar; one cup water; two eggs and two and one-half cups flour with 2 teaspoons baking powder. Bake in layers and put together with white boiled icing.
    MRS. M. R. BIGGS.

Black Cake.—Two cups of molasses; one cup brown sugar; one cup of butter; from three to five eggs (as you can afford); one-half cup of sour milk or cold coffee; two full teaspoonfuls of soda; one teaspoonful of cinnamon, one-half pound of raisins; currants and citron.
    MRS. C. C. BABBIDGE.

Brown Stone Front Cake.—One cup brown sugar; one-half cup of butter; 2 eggs; one-half cup sour milk; 2 cups of flour; 1 even teaspoon of soda. **Dark Part.**—One cup grated chocolate; one-half cup of brown sugar; yolk of 1 egg; one-half cup of sweet milk; 1 tablespoon of vanilla. Boil together and pour hot into batter made as above. Bake in two parts and put together with boiled frosting.

MRS. ELIZABETH B. JACKSON.

Black Walnut Cake.—Two cups of sugar; 1 cup of butter; whites of five eggs; three and one-half cups of flour; 1 cup of sweet milk; teaspoonful of vanilla; 2 teaspoonfuls of baking powder. Filling: Three cups brown sugar; one-half cup of milk; butter size of a walnut. Let the sugar, butter and milk boil up till almost the consistency of molasses, then add nuts. Let boil one minute longer and beat well before spreading on the cake.

MRS. CLIFTON.

Black Chocolate Cake.—One-half cup of butter; 1 cup sugar (scant); one and one-half cups of flour after sifted; one-half cup buttermilk or sour milk; one-half teaspoonful soda dissolved in a little water; one-fourth cake of melted chocolate stirred in 2 eggs.

MRS. ISOM CLEEK.

Cocoanut Cake.—One cup of sugar; one-third cup butter; one-half cup milk; one and one-half cups flour; two teaspoons baking powder; whites of three eggs, beaten to a froth and added last. Stir very little after the eggs are in. Filling: The rind and juice of one lemon; yolk of one egg; one cup powdered sugar; one-half grated cocoanut; a little milk. Cook until thick.

MRS. CROOKS.

Brownie Cake—Dark Part.—Two-thirds cup ground chocolate, Baker's fitter; half cup sweet milk; two-thirds cup brown sugar; scant teaspoon cinnamon; 1 scant teaspoon nutmeg. Boil all together for 3 minutes and set aside to cool. **White part.**—One cup of sugar; 1 cup of butter; one-half cup of milk; 3 eggs; two and one-fourth cups of flour; 2 teaspoons baking powder.

MRS. C. A. RIDDLE.

Cream Cake.—Two cups powdered sugar; two-thirds cup butter; 4 eggs; one-half cup sweet milk; one-half teaspoon soda; 1 teaspoon cream tartar; 3 cups flour. Bake in thin layers and when cold, use the following filling: One-half pint milk; 1 small teaspoon cornstarch; 1 egg; 1 teaspoon vanilla; one-half cup sugar. Heat the milk to boiling, stir in the cornstarch after dissolving in a little cold milk; take out a little and mix with the beaten egg and sugar; pour this into the hot milk; stir constantly until quite thick. Cool, flavor and spread on cakes.

MRS. JULIA YOUNG.

Chocolate Cake.—Two cups sugar; 1 cup butter; 2 cups flour; 1 cup mashed potatoes; one-half cup milk; 1 big cup chocolate; 1 teaspoon baking powder; cloves; nutmeg; 1 cup raisins; 4 eggs.

L. H. C.

Chocolate Cake.—Half cup butter; two cups sugar; two cups flour; half cup hot coffee; half cup milk; two teaspoons baking powder; two teaspoons vanilla; two eggs; one square Baker's chocolate; rub butter and sugar to a cream, add the beaten eggs, then the milk; grate chocolate fine, add to the coffee, which should be very hot; stir well and gradually add to the butter, sugar and eggs. Sift powder and flour together; add the flour, beating well, then the vanilla. Bake in one loaf forty minutes in a moderate oven.

N. DUDLEY·

Caramel Cake.—One and one-half cups sugar; one-fourth cup butter, creamed; then add 2 yolks; add gradually 1 cup water and 2 cups flour, and beat five minutes; add 2 teaspoonfuls caramel; one-half cup flour; 2 teaspoonfuls baking powder, and beat good; add whites last. Put together with boiled icing in which 2 or 3 teaspoons caramel have been added. **To Make the Caramel.**—Put sugar in pan and add a little water; let it boil until very brown, then add water and let it boil until like syrup.

MRS. W. F. KING.

Coffee Cake.—One cup of sugar; 1 cup of molasses; 2 cups of raisins; 1 teaspoon of cinnamon; one-fourth of cloves; 1 teaspoon of soda, dissolved in 1 cup of strong black coffee, cold; 5 cups of flour; 3 eggs; 1 cup of butter, creamed with sugar.

MRS. M. A. MCKENZIE.

Surprise Cake.—One and one-half cups of flour; 1 cup of sugar, scant; 1 teaspoon of baking powder; sift it together; butter one-half cup, set on stove to melt in cup; break 2 eggs into cup and fill cup with milk; flavor with vanilla and bake in layers. Add filling with whipped cream.

MRS. FRANK HOFFMAN.

Coffee Cake.—Bake one hour in moderate oven 1 cup of brown sugar; 1 cup of molasses; one-half cup of butter; one-half cup of lard; 1 cup of cold coffee; 1 tablespoon cinnamon, and one of cloves; a dash of nutmeg and vanilla; 2 eggs beaten; one-half pound raisins and currants, mixed; three and one-half cups of flour; 1 teaspoon of soda mixed into molasses.

MRS. J. FRANK SPINNING.

Delicate Spice Cake.—Two-thirds cup melted butter; two-thirds cup sugar; two and one-half cups flour (generous); one egg; two-thirds cup molasses; one cup milk; two small teaspoonfuls baking powder; one tablespoonful vinegar or lemon juice; one tablespoonful mixed spices (cinnamon, cloves, mace and nutmeg); beat the egg well; add molasses, sugar, spices, butter, milk and last the vinegar or juice. Bake in shallow pans.

MRS. CARRIE D. RICE.

Delicate Cake.—One cup sugar; one-half cup butter; two-thirds cup milk; whites of 6 eggs; 3 cups flour; 3 teaspoonfuls baking powder.

MRS. M. R. BIGGS.

Walnut Cakes.—Two cups sugar; 1 cup butter; one-half cup milk; 1 cup nuts; three and one-half cups flour; 3 eggs; 1 teaspoon cinnamon; one-half teaspoon of cloves; 2 teaspoons baking powder; drop in small spoonful on buttered paper. Bake in quick oven.

MRS. M. R. BIGGS.

Dried Apple Cake.—Soak two cups dried apples over night; simmer one hour in one cup molasses, first having been chopped to the size of raisins; add one cup sugar; one cup butter; one cup sweet milk, in which one teaspoonful soda has been dissolved; three good cups flour; 2 eggs; 1 teaspoonful cinnamon; cloves and nutmeg; one cup raisins; one cup currants if you like.

MRS. M. R. ELLIOTT.

Dainty Layer Cake.—Cream 1 cup sugar with half cup butter; add 3 eggs, one at a time, beating each one in thoroughly before adding next; add one-half cup milk; 1 teaspoon vanilla; 2 cups flour, sifted twice before measuring, then again with 2 teaspoons baking powder. Beat batter until smooth.

L. BIGGS.

Sunshine Cake (Very Fine).—Whites of 11 eggs; one and one-half cups sugar; yolks of 3 eggs; 1 cup unsifted flour; 2 teaspoons vanilla; 1 cream tartar into flour; sift 5 times. Beat whites stiff; beat yolks, add to whites, add sugar carefully, flavoring last. Flour mix quickly and turn into ungreased pan. Bake 45 minutes.

L. BIGGS.

Nut Cake.—One and one-half cups sugar; one-half cup butter; 2 yolks; 1 cup milk; 2 cups flour; two and one-half teaspoons baking powder; 1 pound chopped nuts; 2 whites egg beaten stiff; add last.

L. BIGGS.

Devil's Food.—One cup sugar; two-thirds cup butter; one cup milk; two and one-half cups flour; two teaspoonfuls baking powder; one-half teaspoonful soda. Before adding flour add the following hot: One cup sugar; one cup water or milk; one-half bar Baker's chocolate. Filling: Three cups brown sugar; one cup water; cooked until thick; then add one-half cup cream; boil until thick; add chopped nuts. Stir until creamy.

MRS. IDA MORSE.

Easter Cake.—Cream together 1 cup of sugar and one-half cup of butter; one-half cup of water; whites of 8 eggs well beaten with 1 teaspoon of lemon juice; two and one-fourth cups of flour with 2 scant teaspoons of baking powder; add whites of eggs, and flour alternately; stir one way, do not beat. Flavor with vanilla. Bake one hour.

MRS. A. THOMSON.

Chocolate Cake.—One cup of butter; 2 cups of sugar; 1 cups of milk; 5 eggs; leave out whites of three; 4 cups of flour; 2 teaspoons of baking powder in the flour; flavor with vanilla, and bake in four layers. For filling take whites of 3 eggs beaten stiff; one and one-half cups of powdered sugar; six tablespoons grated chocolate.

MRS. FLETCHER J. LIVELY.

French Loaf Cake.—Two cups sugar; one-half cup butter; one cup sweet milk; three cups flour; three eggs; two teaspoonfuls baking powder.

MRS. CARRIE D. RICE.

Fruit Cake.—One cup butter; 2 cups sugar; three and one-half cups flour; 1 cup molasses; 1 cup cream; 4 eggs; 1 pound raisins; citron and currants according to taste; 1 teaspoon soda; spice to taste; juice 1 lemon; one-half pint brandy. Leave out or substitute.

MRS. B. F. J.

Hermits.—One cup of butter; 2 cups of sugar; one-half teaspoon of soda dissolved in four tablespoons of milk; 2 teaspoons of cinnamon; 1 of cloves; 4 eggs; teaspoon of vanilla; half-cup of raisins; cup of walnuts, chopped; 4 cups of flour. Cream butter and sugar, add beaten eggs, spices, soda, then flour; dredge raisins and nuts in flour; drop batter from teaspoon into greased tins. Bake thoroughly.

WILDA BELKNAP.

Ice Cream Cake.—Cream one cupful of sugar and one-half cupful of butter; the yolk of one egg and whites of three; one-half cupful of sweet milk; one and three-fourths cupfuls of flour; one-half teaspoonful of soda and one teaspoonful cream of tartar, or one teaspoonful baking powder. Icing.—Beat the yolks of two eggs, to which add eight tablespoonfuls of powdered sugar; flavor to taste; cut in diamonds, lay on plate with sharp points to center, and a candied cherry on each piece.

MRS. T. Y. SUMNER.

Snow Cake.—One-half cupful of butter; 1 cup sugar; one and one-half cups of flour; one-half cup of sweet milk; whites of four eggs; one teaspoonful baking powder sifted with flour. Flavor to taste.

MRS. T. Y. SUMNER.

Sponge Cake.—Mix one cupful flour with one heaping teaspoonful baking powder; one cupful sugar; 3 eggs, one tablespoonful sweet milk. Flavor and stir briskly. Bake at once.

MRS. T. Y. SUMNER.

Jam Cake.—Three eggs; 1 cup C sugar; 1 cup jam; three-fourths cup butter; 1 teaspoon each cinnamon, allspice; one-half nutmeg; 3 tablespoons sour cream; 1 teaspoon soda; one-half cup flour. (No more.)

L. BIGGS.

Japanese Cake.—Six eggs; 2 cups sugar; 1 cup butter; three and one-half cups flour; one-half cups milk. Cook two layers of this light part and add to the remaining batter 2 teaspoons ground cinnamon; 1 teaspoon ground cloves; 1 teaspoon ground spice; 1 cup chipped raisins. This will make three layers. Filling: One cup boiling water; 2 cups sugar; 1 grated cocoanut: 1 teaspoon cornstarch; grated rind and juice of two lemons. Mix and cook till it will drop from a spoon.

MRS. YOUNG.

Lemon Cake—(Make three layers of cake, not too rich).—Melt a tablespoon of butter and half a cup of sugar over a slow fire, stirring all the time; add the juice and grated rind of one lemon; then stir in two well-beaten eggs and a pinch of salt. Stir and as the mixture begins to thicken remove from the fire. When cool, spread between the cake. This is a semi-transparent tart filling.

H. G. D.

Pound Cake.—Cup and a half butter; two cups sugar; seven eggs; pint and a half of flour; teaspoonful of baking powder; teaspoon extract of nutmeg. Bake in deep, paper-lined cake tins, in a steady oven 50 minutes. Ice to suit.   H. G. D.

Lemon Cake.—Four cups flour (white and clean); 1 cup butter (good butter); 6 eggs (new laid eggs, well beaten); 1 cup sweet milk; 1 large lemon (two if small); 3 cups sugar; 1 teaspoon soda.
>   Bake in pans to please the eye,
>   Round or oblong should you try,
>   One thing note without surprise,
>   The more you make the less they rise.
>   MOTHER DUDLEY.

Lady Baltimore Cake.—Here is a South Carolina recipe for this cake, a favorite in all Southern dining rooms long before Mr. Owen Wister heaped dining room honors upon it: Two-thirds of a cupful of butter; five eggs; two cupfuls of sugar; four cupfuls of flour; one-half cupful of rich milk; two level teaspoonfuls of cream of tartar and one level teaspoonful of soda. Cream half the sugar with the butter, beat the remaining sugar into the yolks of the eggs, and sift the cream of tartar and soda **twice** through the flour; beat the eggs and sugar together with the butter and sugar; add the milk slowly and finally beat in the flour and stiffly beaten whites of the eggs. Flavor half this mixture with rose, and into the other half beat one teaspoonful of powdered cinnamon; one teaspoonful of powdered cloves and one grated nutmeg, and flavor with vanilla, lemon or almond. Bake in four layer-cake pans—two white layers and two spiced layers. **Filling for Lady Baltimore Cake.**—Cut fine one cupful of seeded raisins; shred thin half a citron melon; grate one small cocoanut and blanch three-fourths of a pound of almonds; make an ordinary boiled icing, and into it beat all these ingredients save the almonds. Put the mixture thickly between the layers, and finish top layer—which should be a white one—with sprinkled powdered sugar and the almonds stuck in porcupine-wise. The measuring cups are ordinary coffee cups and are filled **just level.** This is a successful recipe and one easily followed.
>   MRS. HAUER.

Layer Nut Cake.—One cup butter; 2 cups sugar; 3 cups flour; 1 cup sweet milk; 7 eggs, whites and yolks, too; 2 teaspoons baking powder; 1 pint English walnuts. **Filling for Same.**—Three and one-half cups granulated sugar; cream enough to dissolve well. Cook slow until soft ball when dropped in cold water; small cup of nuts in filling.
>   MRS. HUGH LISTER.

Minnehaha Cake.—One-half cup butter; one and one-half cups sugar; three eggs; one cup milk; two and one-half cups flour; two teaspoonfuls baking powder; one teaspoonful vanilla. Mix dry ingredients, cream butter and sugar, add beaten yolks and vanilla, and then alternately milk and flour. Beat well and bake in three layers in quick oven. Put together with lemon filling. **Filling.**—Grated rinds of two lemons, their strained juice; two cups sugar; whites of two eggs; one cup boiling water; two tablespoonfuls flour mixed with cold water; one tablespoonful melted butter. Cook together in double boiler, adding beaten whites last.   MRS. JENNIE PICKETT.

Molasses Fruit Cake.—One cup butter; 1 cup brown sugar, creamed; 2 cups cooking molasses; 1 cup sweet milk, with a teaspoon of soda dissolved in it; 1 tablespoon ginger; 1 tablespoon cinnamon; a little grated nutmeg; now add 4 eggs well beaten and 5 cups sifted flour; 1 cup of raisins; 1 cup of nuts, add these last. Bake in a moderate oven 1 hour if kept well covered. Will keep six months.

Marguerites.—Boil 1 cup of white sugar and one-half cup water till it hairs; put on back of stove; add 5 marshmallows, cut in small pieces, and pour on the white of 2 eggs beaten stiff; add 2 tablespoons cocoanut; 1 cup walnut meats, broken into bits; one-fourth teaspoon vanilla; spread on salted wafers and brown in oven. MRS. J. H. W.

Mocha Cake.—Cream together, one cup of sugar; one-half cup of butter; add 4 eggs well beaten; one-half cup of good, strong coffee, and two cups of flour or more if needed. Bake in three layers. For filling, whip one pint of cream; add to this one cup of chopped walnut meats and one tablespoonful of coffee. This is a very good cake.

Chocolate Pineapple Cake.—Three cups sugar; one cup butter; five eggs; three and one-half cups of flour; one-half cup cold water; two teaspoonfuls baking powder. Bake in layers; spread each layer with a thick icing, then cover with grated pineapple. Place on next layer and treat as before. Cover top and sides with chocolate frosting.
MRS. H. G. D.

Maud S. Cake.—Five eggs; one and one-half cups brown sugar; one-half cup butter; one-half cup sweet milk; one-half cup flour; to this add the chocolate custard, made as follows: 8 tablespoons cholocate; 5 tablespoons granulated sugar; one-half cup sweet milk. Cook until it thickens, beat until cool and stir into cake. Add one and one-half cups flour and 2 teaspoons baking powder, and beat well. **Frosting.**—One cup white sugar; one-half cup sweet milk; boil 8 minutes; add lump of butter, size of an egg, and vanilla. Beat until cool.
MRS. SENTRY.

Nut Cake.—Two cups sugar; 1 cup butter; 1 cup milk; 3 cups flour; whites of 7 eggs; yolks of 3 eggs; 1 scant pint nuts rolled in flour; 2 teaspoons baking powder. Cream filling for the above: 4 cups sugar; one and one-half cups cream. Boil till it forms a soft ball when tested in water. Beat until it is creamy. GERTIE FOSTER.

Nut Cake.—One and a half cups sugar; half cup butter; three-fourths cup milk; two cups flour; two teaspoons baking powder; four eggs, whites only; one and a half pounds English walnuts; cream butter and sugar; add the milk and the flour into which the baking powder has been well mixed. Crack the nuts reserving twenty-five perfect halves for the icing. Chop the nuts fine and stir in just before adding the beaten whites. Bake forty-five minutes. Ice, placing perfect nuts in squares of icing. N. DUDLEY.

Nut Cake.—One cup sweet milk; 2 cups sugar; three-fourths cup butter; 4 cups flour; 5 eggs, beaten separately; 2 teaspoonfuls baking powder: 1 pint English walnuts; 1 pound seeded raisins. Bake one and one-half hours in slow oven. M. L.

61

Prune Cake.—One cup brown sugar; two-thirds cup butter; three eggs; one cup prunes; one-half cup prune juice; one-half cup sour milk; one teaspoonful soda; spices of all kinds; one teaspoonful baking powder with flour. Good.

MRS. CARRIE D. RICE.

Pound Cake.—Sugar, two cups; butter, 1 pound; eggs, 10; flour, 4 cups after sifted; vanilla, 1 teaspoonful; lemon, one teaspoonful. Beat sugar and butter to a cream, add eggs, two at a time, then flour and vanilla and lemon. Bake in one loaf.

MRS. HAYDEN.

Rocks.—One and one-half cups light brown sugar; scant cup butter; three cups flour; large bowl English walnuts (not too fine); one heaping cup raisins; one teaspoonful each soda, cinnamon, nutmeg and cloves. Drop from spoon on buttered tins (about the size of hickory nut). Bake in moderate oven.

MRS. IDA MORSE.

White Cake.—One coffee cup sugar; one-half coffee cup butter; one-half coffee cup milk; one and one-half coffee cups flour; whites of three eggs; two teaspoonfuls baking powder; one-half cup cornstarch. Sift flour, cornstarch and baking powder together and add alternately with the milk. Add last the whites of the eggs, beaten stiff.

MRS. IDA MORSE.

Raised Fruit Cake.—This is an economical, but very good cake. To make it, add to one cupful of granulated sugar, one-half cupful of butter and cream together well. Then stir in the yolks of two eggs alternately with one-half cupful of flour to which add one cupful of bread sponge; the whites of the eggs; one teaspoonful of soda; a cupful of raisins and a cupful of currants; spice with ground cinnamon, cloves and nutmegs, one-half teaspoonful of each. Pour into a large cake tin, let stand to raise for two hours, then bake with moderate heat till quite done.

MRS. H. G. Davis.

Rolled Jelly-cake.—Four eggs; two-thirds cup powdered sugar; two-thirds cup flour (pastry); one-fourth teaspoonful salt; one-half teaspoonful baking powder. Beat egg yolks and sugar light. Add mixed dry ingredients; then the stiffly beaten whites. Mix lightly together. Bake in thin sheet in quick oven. As soon as done turn quickly on a towel wrung out of water, spread with jelly and roll.

MRS. J. V. WRIGHT.

Scripture Cake.—One cup butter, Judges 5:25; three and one-half cups flour, 1 Kings 4:22; 3 cups sugar, Jeremiah 6:20; 2 cups raisins, 1 Samuel 30:12; 2 cups figs, 1 Samuel 30:12; 1 cup almonds, Genesis 43:11; 1 cup water, Genesis 24:17; 6 eggs, Isaiah 10:14; 1 tablespoonful honey, Psalms 19:10; a pinch of salt, Leviticus 2:13; spices to taste, 1 Kings 10:10; 2 tablespoonfuls baking powder, 1 Corinthians 5:6. Follow Solomon's advice for making good boys and you will have a good cake, Proverbs 23:14, or proceed as in ordinary rules for cake making; the raisins should be seeded, the figs chopped, the almonds blanched and sliced and all floured to prevent sinking to the bottom.

MRS. LYDIA WEEDHAM.

Silver or Delicate.—Whites of six eggs; one cupful sweet milk; two cupfuls of sugar; four cupfuls of flour; two-thirds cup butter; flavoring and two teaspoons baking powder. Stir sugar and butter to cream then add the milk and flavoring, part of flour, the beaten whites of eggs then the rest of flour. Bake carefully in tins lined with buttered paper.

MRS. J. H. CROOKS.

Sponge Cake.—Four eggs; 2 cups sugar; 2 cups flour; 2 teaspoonfuls baking powder; 1 cup boiling water; pinch of salt; flavor.

E. TRUE SHATTUCK.

Brown Stone Front Cake.—One cup sugar; one-half cup each butter and sweet milk; 3 eggs; 2 cups flour; 1 teaspoon soda; 1 teaspoon cream of tartar. Black filling: One and one-half cups cocoa; three-fourths cup sweet milk; three-fourths cup sugar; yolk of 1 egg. Cook until thick, stir in the white dough while hot and bake in layers. Put together with frosting.

E. TRUE SHATTUCK.

Sarah Bernhardt Cake.—Whites of eight eggs; three-fourths of a cupful of butter; three and one-half cupfuls of flour; one pound of raisins; two teaspoonfuls of baking powder; one teaspoonful of vanilla. Filling: Three cupfuls of sugar; one cupful of milk; little piece of butter. Let cook until waxy, take from fire, beat hard with two teaspoonfuls of flour. When ready to spread, put a thin layer on cake, sprinkle chopped almonds, then spread grated pineapple, then the cake. Ice thinly.

MRS. CLIFTON.

Dolly Varden Cake—White Part.—One-half cup of butter; 2 cups of flour; 1 teaspoonful of baking powder; 1 cup of sugar; one-half cup of sweet milk; 5 eggs (whites). **Yellow Part.**—One cup sugar; one-half cup sweet milk; 5 eggs (yolks); one-half cup of butter; 2 cups of flour; 1 teaspoonful baking powder; 1 pound of currants. Flavor with nutmeg and cinnamon. Make each part separately as follows: Cream the butter and sugar; beat in the yolks in one part, the whites in the other; add the milk and stir in the flour gradually. The last half cup of flour mix baking powder; add currants and flavoring to yellow part. Bake in layers and put together with the following jelly: One glass of boiled milk; 2 eggs; 1 teaspoonful cornstarch; 1 glass of sugar. Make as you would boiled custard.

MRS. CLIFTON.

Sunshine Cake.—One cup sugar; three-fourths cup flour; whites of seven eggs; yolks of five eggs; 1 teaspoonful of cream tartar; 1 teaspoonful of vanilla. Mix the same as angel food cake, adding yolks of eggs last.

MRS. E. T. SLAYTON.

Spice Cake.—One cup sugar; one-half cup butter; one-half cup sweet milk; two cups flour; two eggs; two tablespoons molasses; one teaspoon cream tartar; one-half teaspoon each soda, cloves, nutmeg; a little salt; a small cup raisins. Bake in layers with frosting between.

MRS. J. H. CROOKS.

J. H. HANER

Lands, Abstracts and Investments

PRINEVILLE, ORE.

Sour Cream Cake.—Two eggs; one cup sugar; one-fourth cup chocolate; one cup cream; one-half teaspoon cinnamon; cloves; nutmeg and salt; one teaspoonful soda in a little hot water; one and one-half cups flour. Flavor with vanilla. Bake in layers or loaf.

MRS. C. W. ELKINS.

Prune Cake.—One cup chopped cooked prunes; one-half cup prune juice; one-half teaspoonful allspice, nutmeg, cinnamon, and cloves; four tablespoonfuls melted butter; yolks three eggs; one heaping cup sugar; one teaspoonful soda in a little warm water; two and one-half cups flour. Put everything together and stir but do not beat. Bake in layers or loaf.

MRS. C. W. ELKINS.

Apple Sauce Cake.—Two cups apple sauce (without sugar); two cups sugar; one cup butter; two scant teaspoonfuls soda beaten into apple sauce and then beaten to a cream with butter and sugar; then add four well-beaten eggs; four cups flour; one cup raisins; one cup nuts; one-fourth cup chocolate, and spices to taste. Bake in loaf.

MRS. C. W. ELKINS.

Burnt Leather Cake.—To one-half cup butter creamed add gradually one and one-half cups sugar; one cup water; yolks of two eggs; two cups flour, and beat five minutes; add three tablespoonfuls syrup; one teaspoonful vanilla; two teaspoonfuls of baking flour in one-half cup of flour; whites of three eggs, beaten but not too light. Bake in quick oven. Filling: One cup sugar; four tablespoonfuls boiling water. Cook until threads, then pour over well beaten whites of two eggs; add one tablespoonful syrup; one-half teaspoonful vanilla. Beat until cold. Syrup: One cup brown sugar; stir constantly over fire until it smokes, remove and add one-half cup boiling water. Stir until it is like syrup.

MRS. C. W. ELKINS.

Marshmallow Filling for Cakes.—Six eggs (whites only); their weight in granulated sugar; whip eggs in granulated sugar; whip eggs a little, then add the sugar gradually and whip until very light; then place bowl over steam and continue to beat until stiff and glossy, when remove and beat until cool. Ice the layers of cake, top and bottom, in order that marshmallows may be thoroughly moistened. The marshmallows should be cut into four pieces with scissors and if at all dry should be thoroughly steamed before laid in the iced layers. Twelve marshmallows.

Chocolate Cream Filling.—One-half cake chocolate grated; two-thirds cup of milk; one-half cup of sugar; 1 tablespoon butter; 1 pinch of salt; 1 teaspoon vanilla. Boil gently till thick.

MRS. C. J. JOHNSON.

Pineapple Filling.—One and one-half cups sugar and juice from can of pineapple cooked till it begins to thicken; then add chopped pineapple and cook till it hairs well, stirring often to prevent burning. When it hairs well pour it over the well beaten whites of 2 eggs and beat till cool.

MRS. JOHN WIGLE.

65

White Cake.—One cup of butter creamed with two cups of sugar; the whites of eight eggs beaten; one cup of milk; three cups of flour; one teaspoon of baking powder. Flavor with vanilla or lemon. Using the yolks makes a fine yellow cake.

MRS. C. I. WINNEK.

White Cake.—One-half cup butter; 1 cup sugar; whites of five eggs; 1 teaspoonful lemon juice; 2 scant cups of flour; 2 teaspoonfuls baking powder slightly rounded; one and a half teaspoonfuls mixed extracts; one-half cup milk.

DOMESTIC SCIENCE TEACHER.

Blackberry Cake.—Sugar, 1 cup; butter, one-half cup; eggs, 2; sour milk, three-fourths cup; soda, 2 teaspoonfuls; allspice, 1 teaspoonful; cloves, 1 teaspoonful; cinnamon, 1 teaspoonful; nutmeg, a little; blackberries, 1 cup; use judgment as to flour.

MILDRED JOHNSON.

Cocoanut Filling.—One cup cocoanut; 1 cup sugar; 1 cup milk; 2 eggs. Cook all together 5 minutes.

MRS. C. J. JOHNSON.

Pendleton Junior College, Academy, and School of Commerce, and School of Music

FACULTY

Rev. W. H. Bleakney, A.B., Ph.D., Science, Philosophy
Rev. R. G. White, A.B., B.D., Mathematics, Dean of Men
Belle W. Wallace, A.B., Greek, Latin
Alvin E. Gronewald, Ph.B., French, German, Spanish
Mrs. Anna Z. Crayne, A.B., Domestic Science, English, Dean of Women
Richard Mayberry, B.Acc., Commercial Studies
Harriet Esther Young, Department of Music

For Information, Address **Pendleton Junior College**
PENDLETON, OREGON

SPECIALS

SPECIALS

DAINTY DISHES AND ICES

"An't please your Honour," quoth the peasant,
"This same dessert is very pleasant."

Banana Sherbet.—One quart boiling water; white of one egg; juice of one orange; 1 pint of sugar; 3 bananas, sliced thin; juice of one lemon. Pour boiling water on the sugar, orange and lemon juice. When nearly cold strain and add sliced bananas and beat whites of the egg and freeze. This makes three pints of sherbet.

MRS. CROOKS.

Bisque Glace.—One pint of cream whipped; whites of two eggs, beaten; bar sugar to sweeten; one-half teaspoonful of vanilla; juice of one lemon; whip all together, put into two one-pound baking powder cans; pack in ice and salt for three hours. After placing lids on cans dip in to prevent salt water from getting in cans. Berries or fruit added makes a delicious flavor.

MRS. C. I. WINNEK.

California Orange Sherbet.—Juice of 4 oranges, 2 lemons; one and a half cups of sugar; 1 quart of water; whites of 2 eggs. Mix all but eggs together and strain. Freeze until it thickens slightly, add the eggs, beaten to a stiff froth and freeze.

LORENE WINNEK.

Lemon Sherbet.—Eight pounds sugar, granulated; 6 quarts water; whites of 1 dozen eggs; 2 dozen lemons. Boil sugar and water together, then let cool; drop whites of eggs in (unbeaten), strain before freezing.

MRS. HUGH LISTER.

Ice Cream.—Eight eggs, beaten separately; 3 cups of sugar, stirred in the yolks; have scalded 1 quart of new milk; pour over the eggs and sugar; beat the whites stiff and stir in; put on the stove and scald 20 minutes or until thick as custard; cool; add 9 teaspoonfuls of vanilla and 3 pints of rich cream; strain and freeze.

JENNIE KING.

Ice Cream.—For 1 gallon ice cream. Two and one-half cups sugar; 8 eggs; 1 quart good cream and sufficient fresh milk to make the gallon. Scald about 2 quarts milk, add sugar and eggs beaten light. Cook in double boiler until it thickens a little. Flavor well with vanilla and when cold add cream and freeze.

MRS. J. H. WIGLE.

69

Delicious Baked Apples.—Peel, halve and core good tart apples, enough for six or eight people, and place in a granite baking pan; chop 1 can of pineapple; pour it and the juice over the apples and add 1 cup of sugar or a little more if apples are very tart; add a little water and bake in a slow oven until all cooked down thick and serve with whipped cream.

MRS. J. H. WIGLE.

Lemon Ice.—Three pints of milk; 1 pint cream; juice of 4 lemons; three-fourths cup sugar; whites of 4 eggs. Mix the milk, cream and one-half the sugar together, freeze until like slush, then add the rest of the sugar into which is stirred the lemon juice and beaten whites of 4 eggs.

MRS. IDA MORSE.

Lemon Ice.—Roll 1 dozen lemons in some sugar, on hard table; extract the oil; squeeze the juice from lemons; then take 5 quarts hot water and add 2 cups sugar to each quart; set on stove, boil and skim; when clear add lemon and lemon sugar. Beat whites of 10 eggs and add just before freezing. MRS. S. N. WILKINS.

Pineapple or Strawberry Mousse.—Chop a can of pineapple very fine; put on stove with cup of sugar and juice of pineapple. Cook about ten minutes and when cool add juice of half a lemon. Take about the same amount of thick cream and whip. Pour fruit in freezer or can and chill; add whipped cream, stir well together; pack with ice and salt and let stand for about three hours. Extra fine. Crushed strawberries either fresh or canned are good.

MRS. J. H. WIGLE.

Marshmallow Dainty.—Whites of six eggs beaten to stiff froth; two level tablespoons sugar; one tablespoon gelatine dissolved in tablespoon of cold water; add four tablespoons boiling hot water; let come to a boil gradually; add two eggs; flavor to taste; divide mixture, add half stick ground chocolate to one part; spread in layers in deep dish. Serve with whipped cream and walnuts. MRS. CROOKS.

Orange Charlotte.—One-third box of gelatine; one-third cup of cold water; one-third cup of boiling water; one cup of sugar; juice of one lemon; one cup of orange juice and pulp; whites of three eggs; soak the gelatine in the cold water till soft; add the boiling water, sugar and lemon juice, strain and add orange juice and a little of grated rind; cool in pan of ice water and when it begins to harden beat in the stiffly beaten whites of eggs. Serve with a custard made of the yolks of eggs; 1 pint of milk; 3 heaping tablespoonfuls of sugar and a little salt. Flavor to taste, or it is fine cut in little cubes and served with whipped cream. M. BRINK.

Tutti Frutti.—Bake a sponge cake in a shallow bread pan; heap fresh sliced peaches, or strawberries, or canned ones, and add whipped cream. Cake should be served, cut in squares and each plate arranged by itself. For cakes, beat 3 eggs with 1 cup sugar very light; 1 teaspoon baking powder; one and a half cups flour; vanilla flavoring. Add last one-half cup boiling water. MRS. J. H. W.

70

CONFECTIONERY

"The sweetest story ever told."

Almond Candy.—Two cupfuls of white sugar; one and one-half cupfuls of sweet milk. Boil until it will crisp in water like molasses candy. Add one-half cupful of blanched almonds, perfectly dry.

BEULAH CROOKS.

Cream Dates.—Boil one and one-half cupfuls of sugar and three-fourths of a cupful of sweet milk; add one-half teaspoonful of butter. Boil about ten minutes. Let it cool; when lukewarm beat, adding a teaspoonful of lemon juice. When it becomes a soft, creamy substance, have ready seeded dates; fill with this cream and serve.

MRS. CLIFTON.

Cream Candy.—Six cups white sugar; one-fourth teaspoon cream tartar; 1 lump of glucose the size of a big egg. By keeping the hand wet with cold water the glucose can be easily pinched off. Water enough to dissolve. Set on back of stove until all is melted, stirring every now and then; place kettle where it will boil quickly; be careful not to shake the kettle and never stir it after it is once heated. Let boil until it forms a soft ball in water and in testing care should be taken not to stir the contents of the kettle, dipping a little from the top. When done remove from fire and pour into earthen or granite bowl; do not scrape or drain the kettle or it will make grainy candy. Let candy cool until milk warm, stir candy with big spoon until it is thick and milky looking. Take out on a marble slab or molding board moistened with water. This must be done quickly or candy will grain. Knead like you would light bread, flavor with preferred flavoring, and pinch off little bits and mold into shape, pressing a walnut meat on some, others may be rolled in chopped nuts or cocoanut; others molded and set away over night for chocolate creams. Remove pits from dates and stuff with some of the cream. For four or five dozen creams break up one small package of bitter chocolate, shave off a little paraffine; be careful to not use too much, as it will taste, and not enough it will not harden. Put in double boiler and when hot dip molded candy one at a time in it. Drain well and lay on greased paper. All the candy, when molded, should be placed on greased paper. When molding, if the candy is inclined to harden, keep covered with a napkin moistened with hot water. It is better to have two to handle the cream when putting it on the board, for if not at the correct stage it will harden. Great care should be taken to not stir the candy, and to let it cool before handling, as these two things are the secret of good cream candy.

MRS. J. H. WIGLE.

Cocoanut Candy.—Two cups milk; 1 cup sugar; 1 cup cocoanut. Boil milk and sugar 20 minutes, stir in cocoanut and let come to a boil. Remove and stir until thick and creamy.

MARION RICE.

Divinity Fudge.—Two cups sugar; one-half cup syrup; one-half cup water. Boil together until it hardens in cold water. Then stir in the beaten whites of two eggs and beat until cool. Add vanilla and nuts and pour into buttered pans.

MARION RICE.

Fudge.—Three cups sugar; one-half cup cream; butter size of walnut; 4 squares chocolate; vanilla.

RUTH EVANS.

Fudge.—Two cups granulated sugar; 1 cup brown sugar; 1 cup milk; 2 tablespoonfuls butter; 2 squares chocolate; 1 cup chopped nuts. Boil all ingredients (omitting nuts) together until mixture forms soft ball when dropped in water. Set aside carefully, removing spoon. Do not disturb until cold. Beat and work until creamy. Turn out in buttered pans.

MRS. CLIFTON.

Marshmallows.—Boil 2 cups sugar with 10 tablespoonfuls of water until it balls; flavor with vanilla; dissolve 2 tablespoonfuls gelatine in 9 of water; pour into the boiling syrup and beat for 20 minutes; pour into pan lined with oiled paper. When cool and firm, turn out on board sprinkled with powdered sugar and cut in squares.

OLIVE J. CARLTON.

Marshmallow Candy.—Two cups sugar; 6 tablespoons water; boil until it hairs; have two tablespoons Knox gelatine soaking in 6 tablespoons cold water; pour syrup over gelatine and beat until too stiff to beat. Then pour into square mould and cut in squares when well set and roll each piece in powdered sugar.

X.

Mexican Pinoche.—Three cups brown sugar; 1 cup cream. Cook till it forms soft ball. Take off stove, add 1 cup pecan or walnuts broken small. Flavor with vanilla. Beat until creamy and drop on buttered paper.

KATE WILLIAMSON.

Sea Foam.—Three and one-half cups brown sugar; one and one-half cups water. Boil until it forms a very soft ball in cold water; Beat whites of 2 eggs and pour first mixture over them slowly, stir very hard. Add vanilla

CELIA NELMS.

Nugat.—Five cups cane sugar; 1 cup glucose; 1 cup hot water; whites of 5 eggs; 1 cup almonds (more better); flavor to taste. Mix sugar, glucose, and water and boil to 258 degrees F. Cool syrup while beating the eggs very stiff. Then pour syrup over whites. Add nuts last. Pour into loaf pans lined with oiled paper.

MRS. W. F. KING.

72

Marshmallow.—Four cups sugar; 13 tablespoonfuls water. Boil together until it forms a soft ball, test in water. Add 1 tablespoonful or 1 box of Knox's gelatine, soaking in 12 tablespoonfuls of cold water while sugar boils. Pour syrup over gelatine and beat until very stiff. Pour into tins dusted with powdered sugar and let set.

Mrs. W. F. King.

Nut Macaroons.—Chop fine, hickory nuts, pecans or walnuts; make frosting as for cakes, stir in meats, putting in enough to make it easy to handle; flour the hands and make the mixture into balls the size of nutmegs; lay on buttered tins, leaving room to spread, and bake in a quick oven.

Beulah Crooks.

Ogontz's Fudge.—Two cups brown sugar; 1 cup white sugar; one-half cup water or milk; butter size of a small egg. When melted stir in 1 cup of chocolate. Stir constantly and cook till it forms a soft ball in water. Then add 1 teaspoon vanilla, stir till it grains, put in buttered pan and mark in squares.

Mrs. C. S. Edwards.

Peppermints.—One and one-half cups sugar; one-half cup boiling water; 3 drops oil peppermint. Put sugar and water into a granite saucepan and stir until sugar is dissolved. Boil ten minutes; remove from fire, add peppermint, and beat until of right consistency. Drop from tip of spoon on slightly buttered paper.

Lorene Winnek.

Pinoche Candy.—Four cups brown sugar; 2 cups syrup; one and one-half cups cream or milk; butter size of egg; chocolate to suit taste; 1 large cup of walnuts. Stir while cooking, add nuts and chocolate just before done.

Robert Lister.

White Pinoche.—Three cups white sugar, with 1 cup cream; then let boil 12 minutes; then pour in 1 tablespoon of vanilla and 1 cup of walnuts. Stir until it begins to harden and put in pan and cut in squares.

X.

Sea Foam.—Three cups of brown sugar; 1 cup of water; 1 tablespoon of vinegar. Boil until it will make quite a firm ball in water. Then pour slowly into it the beaten whites of two eggs, beating all the while. Then add one cup of shredded cocoanut or nut meats if preferred; drop on buttered paper and let cool.

Mona Shipp.

Stuffed Dates.—Make a cut the entire length of date and remove stones; fill cavities with castanea nuts, English walnuts, or blanched almonds, and shape in original form. Roll in powdered sugar. Pile in rows on a small plate covered with a doily. If castanea nuts are used, with sharp knife cut off the brown skin which lies next to the shell.

Lorene Winnek.

Pinoche.—Three cups brown sugar; one-half cup butter; 1 cup cream; 1 cup walnuts chopped fine, added just before taking off the stove; flavor with lemon or vanilla.

BEATRICE JOHNSON.

Six Minute Candy.—Two cups sugar; one-half cup milk; butter the size of two walnuts; chocolate to taste. Boil just six minutes after it commences to boil all over; stir while boiling. Turn out and cut when partly cold.

MRS. S. J. NEWSOM.

Taffy.—Three cups white sugar; two-thirds cup lukewarm water; one-half teaspoon cream tartar; one-half teaspoon corn starch. Boil till it can be picked up nicely when dropped in cold water. Flavor to taste just before taking from fire. Pour out into buttered tins and pull when cool enough.

CELIA NELMS.

CANNED FRUIT
PRESERVES AND JELLIES

BOTH SIDES.

He—"Can you cook?"
She—"Can you provide the things wherewith to cook?"

Canned Strawberries.—Two cups sugar with enough hot water to dissolve and cover well the bottom of a large preserving pan. Cook till it hairs well, the thicker the better, so as not to burn; add one and a half boxes strawberries, hulled and mashed; cook till fruit looks clear; seal in quart jars. The above is sufficient for 1 quart. Berries should be hulled and put in sieve or colander, then held under faucet to wash and dropped immediately into syrup, and when cold wrapped in several thicknesses of paper and kept in dark place.

·Mrs. John Wigle.

Pear Preserves.—Peel, core and quarter Fall Bartlett pears, which are the best for preserves; weigh and take three-quarters as much sugar as fruit; use enough water to dissolve sugar; cook till thick; add pears and cook till pears are clear; a little ginger root pounded and tied in a bag adds very much to the flavor. If you wish the pears a rich dark color, cook slowly a long time. Bartletts will not color much. Sweet fruit, like pears, or ground cherries, may be cooked a long time without injury, but fruits with much acid will grow strong, especially peaches, plums and strawberries.

Mrs. J. H. W.

Jellies and Jams.—In making all jellies except apple, mash fruit and cover with cold water; cook fruit till tender; pour in sack or bag and let drain, but do not squeeze or you will have cloudy jelly; use heaping bowl of juice to scant bowl of sugar, and boil till a little placed on a cool plate is thick; about 15 or 20 minutes is usually enough, but one should test it frequently; when right test is reached pour into hot glasses and set away to cool; cover with paper when cold. The best apple jelly is made from the peelings. Proceed as above, and before pouring into glasses drop one rose geranium leaf in each glass to give a spicy flavor to the jelly. Do not let the jelly bag drip too long. Take pulp and rub through a coarse sieve; measure as for jelly and cook in same way, testing, and when thick it may be sealed in jars or will keep well in open crocks. Care should be taken in cooking pulp, as it burns easily. Skim both jelly and jam while cooking.

Committee.

Delicious Water Melon Preserves.—Cut off rind, cut in pieces, weigh, add a heaping teaspoon each of salt and pulverized alum to two gallons of rinds; let stand until salt and alum dissolve, fill the kettle with cold water, and place on top of stove where it will slowly come to boiling point, covering with large plate so as to keep rinds under boil until they can be easily pierced with fork; drain them from the water, and put into a syrup previously prepared as follows: Bruise and tie in a muslin bag 4 ounces of ginger root, and boil in 2 or 3 pints of water until it is strongly flavored. At the same time boil in a little water until tender, in another pan, 3 or 4 sliced lemons. Make a syrup of the sugar equal to weight of fruit, and the water in which the lemons and ginger root were boiled; add the rinds and slices of lemon to this and boil slowly half to three-quarters of an hour. Citrons may be prepared in same way.

MRS. JOHN WIGLE.

Sun Strawberry Preserves.—Equal parts of sugar and fruit; set over night; do not stir until morning; do not mash berries; cook 5 or 8 minutes, then put into granite pans 1 or 1½ inches deep; set in sun from 3 to 5 days; cover with cloth to prevent dust from falling into fruit.

MRS. A. THOMSON.

PICKLES

"The turnpike road to people's hearts I find
Lies through their mouths, or I mistake mankind."

Apple Chutney.—Two pounds brown sugar, two quarts vinegar (less if apples are juicy), four and one-half pounds good cooking apples, weighed after coring and peeling, one and one-half pounds raisins, seeded, four ounces salt, one ounce mustard seed, one ounce grated ginger, one-quarter pound cayenne. Cook all together, like jam, over slow fire. Some prefer celery seed. Leave in kettle and stir every day for a week; then seal in medium neck bottles.

MRS. COLLINS W. ELKINS.

Dill Pickles.—Wipe and pack in jar or keg good-sized cucumbers, a little dill and small red peppers or large green ones cut in pieces, in layers till required amount is used. To nineteen cups water add one cup good sour vinegar, one cup salt; bring to boil, skim and cool till it is just milk-warm; pour over cucumbers; put cloth next to pickles and plate, then weight with rock; set in warm place. A scum will gather on cloth, which must be kept clean. Ready for use in a few weeks.

MRS. J. H. WIGLE.

Green Tomato Soy.—Two gallons tomatoes, sliced without peeling, twelve good-sized onions, two quarts vinegar, one quart sugar, two tablespoons salt, two tablespoons ground mustard, two tablespoons black pepper, one tablespoon whole allspice. 1 tablespoon cloves; mix all together, stew until tender; watch carefully that slices do not break; seal in glass jars.

MRS. HARPER.

Mixed Pickles.—One quart each of small cucumbers (or large ones sliced), small (and sliced) onions, sliced cabbage, about one-half inch in thickness, green beans, sliced carrots, sliced green tomatoes and cauliflower. Soak over night (each in separate vessel) in strong brine; pour off and wash several times in cold water; place in jars (those with large mouths preferred), mixing the various vegetables in an artistic or pleasing manner, according to the individual taste. Put in in alternate layers, with the following spices: Cinnamon sticks, white mustard seed, whole cloves, whole allspice, and a few bay leaves. The last layer to be of the spices, on top of which place several pieces of horseradish. To one quart of good cider vinegar, add four tablespoons brown sugar and four tablespoons olive oil; heat to boiling point (do not let boil) and pour over the filled jar and seal up.

ADA B. MILLICAN.

Chicago Hot.—One peck ripe tomatoes, drained over night, six onions, six red peppers, three heads celery, all chopped fine, one-half cup salt, two-thirds cup brown sugar, one-half cup white mustard seed, and one quart vinegar.

MRS. IDA MORSE.

Mustard Pickles.—One quart large cucumbers, 1 quart small cucumbers, 2 quarts onions (small), four heads cauliflower, six green peppers, 1 quart green tomatoes, 1 gallon vinegar, 1 pound Colman's mustard, two cups brown sugar, two cup flour, one ounce tumeric. Sift sugar, flour, mustard and tumeric together; have vinegar heated, and pour slowly over the mixture, making a smooth paste; then cook and pour on heated vegetables.

MRS. E. J. BURROWS.

Pickles (No. 1).—Place small cucumbers in brine that will bear an egg; let them stand for thirty-six hours; drain, and cover with boiling vinegar, and stand for twenty-four or thirty-six hours; pour off vinegar, pack pickles in jars and cover with spiced vinegar. It is not necessary to cover vinegar.

Spiced Vinegar.—To a gallon of good vinegar add a handful of cinnamon bark, 1 pound of brown sugar, one-half pint of salt, one small box of mustard, two ounces each of cloves, mace, allspice, ground ginger and black pepper, not ground, and white mustard seed: also three dozen small onions, one pod green pepper, horseradish ground to taste; add a little tumeric powder to prevent mould.

LIZZIE JACKSON.

Sliced Cucumber Pickles.—Six dozen large cucumbers, sliced, in salt water, one-quarter peck small onions, six red peppers, 1 gallon vinegar, 1 pound brown sugar, one-quarter pound mustard seed, three-quarter pound ground mustard, one ounce celery seed. Heat the vinegar and spice to boiling; then mix mustard with cold vinegar, pour in boiling vinegar and let boil; then put in vinegar and seeds; pour over pickles boiling hot.

MRS. IDA MORSE.

Sweet Pickle Vinegar, Spiced.—1 quart best cider vinegar to three pints sugar (Extra C is the best; if not to be had, use white) to each gallon of fruit, two teaspoons whole cloves, four tablespoons cinnamon in sticks, one tablespoon allspice, whole. Heat all together, skim and pour over fruit while hot. The old rule said reheat vinegar every other morning for two weeks, the last time heating fruit in vinegar. A quicker way is to bring vinegar, sugar and spice to a boiling heat, put in fruit and cook till fruit is easily pierced with a fork; skim out fruit and place in jar; boil vinegar a few minutes and pour over fruit; let stand three days, reheat and pour over fruit; watch fruit, and if scum rises and syrup appears whitish, boil, skim and pour over fruit again. This should keep a year or more if properly done. Peaches, pears, prunes, plums or cherries are nice. Peel pears, and if large cut in half; rub peaches well with a cloth and stick prunes or plums with a fork before heating in the vinegar.

MRS. J. H. WIGLE.

Pickles (No. 2).—1 gallon vinegar, 1 quart sugar, allspice and cinnamon, red pepper; boil pickles and all together fifteen minutes; seal while hot in half-gallon jars.

OLLIE ELKINS STEWART.

Piccalilli.—One-half peck green tomatoes, two heads cabbage, nine large onions, one dozen good-sized cucumbers, one-half dozen green peppers, one-quarter pound mustard seed. Chop all fine; make a strong brine of salt water and boil your chopped piccalilli in it about five minutes; remove from the fire and press out every drop of the brine; then mix in the mustard seed and put all in a large stone jar; boil a gallon of pickling vinegar and pour over hot. It is fit to use as soon as cold, and will keep a year.

BLANCHE MICHEL.

Ripe Tomato Pickles.—Place well-washed grape leaves in bottom of stone jar; pack in medium-sized, perfectly smooth, ripe tomatoes; sprinkle with white mustard seed; then another layer of grape leaves, then a layer of tomatoes and mustard seed until the jar is filled; cover with cold cider vinegar; put a plate on to keep tomatoes under the vinegar. When wanted, cut tomatoes crosswise in halves and fill with sugar.

MRS. IDA MORSE.

Stuffed Chili Peppers.—One dozen chili peppers; make an incision in side of pepper and remove seeds; soak in strong brine over night; chop one head of cabbage, and one-half dozen onions very fine, and season to taste with some of the chili pepper and white mustard seed; fill the peppers and sew up the incisions; place in stone or granite vessel, with layers of the following spices: Cinnamon sticks, whole cloves and whole allspice; on top place several pieces of horseradish. To one quart of cider vinegar, add four tablespoons brown sugar and six tablespoons olive oil; put on stove and let come to boil, and pour over peppers and seal up. If not sealed heat vinegar to boiling point and pour over peppers for six consecutive days.

ADA B. MILLICAN.

Tomato Relish.—One peck green tomatoes, peeled and chopped, one tablespoon salt; put to drain over night; add two cups celery, chopped, two cups sugar, two ounces white mustard seed, one-half teaspoonful each cloves, cinnamon and spice, one quart vinegar; cook one hour.

E. TRUE SHATTUCK.

Tomato Catsup.—One box ripe tomatoes, three or four small onions; cut fine and cook; then strain and add to this juice one pint vinegar, three cups sugar, one tablespoon mixed pickle spice; put in cloth; dust in pepper and celery salt; one tablespoon Colman's mustard, one-half cup salt; add one stick cinnamon, one large tablespoon each of cloves and allspice; put in cloth; do this to keep the natural color of tomatoes.

MRS. E. J. BURROWS.

Tomato Pickles or Chowchow.—One peck green tomatoes, six large onions, sliced; sprinkle with one cupful salt and let stand over night; then drain, add two quarts of water and a little vinegar—about one cup if strong, or less. Boil fifteen minutes, then drain; add to the pickles two pounds sugar, two quarts vinegar, two tablespoons cloves, allspice, ginger and cinnamon, one of pepper; boil fifteen minutes, or a little longer; add more sugar if you like. This will be found to be very nice.

Mrs. T. Y. Sumner.

SPECIALS